MEET ME IN THE
DOGHOUSE

Bruce David Colen

MEET ME
IN THE
DOGHOUSE

Doubleday & Company, Inc.

Garden City, New York   1973

ISBN: 0-385-05827-6
Library of Congress Catalog Card Number 72–84899
Copyright © 1973 by Bruce David Colen. All Rights Reserved
PRINTED IN THE UNITED STATES OF AMERICA
FIRST EDITION

FOR

Eszter Haraszty —
A woman who makes beauty.

B.D.C.

ERRATA

The following photo credits were inadvertently left out of the first edition:

Gordon Parks, *Life* © 1962; Time, Inc.—8, 16

Hans Namuth—17

Eszter Haraszty—2, 4, 5, 6, 13, 15, 20, 21, 25, 26

Howard Gordon—11, 12, 14, 22, 27, 28, 29, 30, 31

Mary Frampton, Los Angeles *Times*—22

Bruce Colen—1, 3, 7, 9, 10, 18, 23, 24

Contents

Author's Note

Thirteen years ago I was living a messy bachelor's life on New York's East Fifty-sixth Street. My do-it-yourself skills were limited to pressing an elevator button and opening an incinerator chute. I accepted the city for what it was—a stimulating, feverish, filthy, and often sadly empty place. New York is a forty-hour town. A great place to work; but unless you are a computer, survival calls for plugging in elsewhere.

My yearnings for the country were sublimated by Jean Renoir films and Hal Borland's nature studies on the editorial page of the New York *Times*. Lovely, long green weekends at other people's homes in Connecticut or on Long Island made returning to town harder and harder.

From Monday to Friday the closest I came to the animal world was sharing the sidewalks with dogs and a stuffed American Eagle which glowered down from a perch behind my boss's desk. Hubbell Robinson, the last of CBS's creative Programing Vice Presidents, is part Mohawk and I think he kept that bird over his shoulder as a reminder of a proud past and of a present and future that took fighting.

This fragmented way of life was suddenly made whole by a chance meeting with an even-tempered Great Dane and her temperamental Hungarian mistress. Only at a New York cocktail party can you find yourself cornered with a harlequin Dane. We were running out of small talk, when a very attractive woman walked over. "I hope you're not trapped. That's my dog, Dorka; it means Dorothy in Hungarian. I'm Eszter Haraszty." For the next six months the three of us were inseparable. Eszter has always said I married her for Dorka and her Calder sculpture. A foolish joke. I have never liked mobiles.

Born in Hungary of a father whose hobby was espaliering peach and pear trees, and of a mother who specialized in bending daughters, Eszter was trained at the University of Budapest as a costume and stage designer. She physically survived the German siege, the Russian occupation, and the American bombings (the last killed her parents), only to be spiritually defeated by the mediocrity of the "new" Hungary once the Russians had returned. Forty pounds underweight but one hundred lighter in spirit, she arrived in America in 1947. Her sister and brother-in-law had established a beachhead, he as press attaché for the first and last democratic Hungarian ambassador to the United States, she as the worst driver with diplomatic immunity in the history of the Washington police force.

After a month of lunching on banana splits and a nightly can of cocktail peanuts with cream while she did her English lessons in bed, Eszter headed for New York heavier and wiser in the ways of her new country.

Molnár, who was living at the Plaza then, offered to open some theatrical doors for this daughter of an old friend; but, at the same time, the Broadway unions opened their palms and Eszter did not have the money for initiation fees or dues.

"I became an interior designer. I sink you have an expression, 'There is more than vun vay to vash a mule.'"

This was my first E.H. malaprop. They enchant me; but after years of listening to daily slips, an accent thicker than a Székely *gulyás'*, an asexual approach to genders, and a proclivity for inverted sentences, I very often become confused and exhausted. If in the following pages Eszter's speech pattern is not always faithfully recorded, it was an intentional act of self-preservation.

This is the story of Eszter and Dorka and the good life which befell all several dozen of us. It is not meant to prove anything; but as I read the final galley proofs, it occurs to me that it is too late to change one's life only if you live it alone.

B.D.C.

June 1, 1972

MEET ME IN THE
DOGHOUSE

1

No Dogs Allowed

Both Eszter and I had been to California before on brief business trips; nevertheless, I wanted this postmarriage arrival in our new home territory to be something special. It was. We stood outside Union Station, waiting for a taxi, in one of the heaviest rainstorms in the history of Los Angeles.

Rain is one of several natural phenomena, along with earthquakes, landslides, and fires, which Californians refuse to acknowledge, except when the state legislature in Sacramento decides to petition Washington for Flood Relief grants. The collective California psyche would be much less schizophrenic if somebody, preferably Norman Chandler, owner of the Los Angeles *Times,* came out and faced the fact that from February to mid-June the weather in the Los Angeles Basin is a potpourri of fog, smog, and eight-and-a-half-month-pregnant clouds that can't make up their mind whether or not to drop their litter. Instead, there is the diurnal front-page weather report: Early morning haze giving way to sunshine.

The radio and television networks carry on the same sham. Not once, but six to eight times an hour: "Another beautiful day for all our listeners. The temperature at Civic Center is

now sixty-four degrees with a high of eighty-two expected."
These cheery words are heard by the freeway motorist squint-
ing through a fog-banked windshield on his way to work and
by his wife at home who immediately makes her school-bound
child don a raincoat. In 1967, while stalled at a flooded inter-
section, I heard a radio announcer forecast, "A slight chance of
drizzles in the Basin today." The following morning the newspapers carried the tragic account of a man who had been
swept into a storm drain and drowned on Coldwater Canyon,
a Beverly Hills thoroughfare fronted by homes costing $160,-
000 to $350,000.

There is one exception to this weather blindness on the
West Coast. San Franciscans not only admit that ten months
of the year the Bay Area is subject to monsoons, but they are
proud of the inundations and broadcast, near and far, the rain,
wind, and fog statistics. Masochism? Hardly. How else could
America's most beautiful city avoid a population explosion?

Back to Union Station, standing ankle deep in water, *on the
sidewalk,* waiting for a taxi to take us to the place I had
rented on my last trip to the Coast for Hubbell Robinson Productions. It was meant to be a halfway house until we decided
if we really liked California and wanted to settle down in a
home of our own. I was very proud of my find and most anxious to see if Eszter shared my enthusiasm. It was the pool
house on the old Al Jolson estate. Over the past years, according to a first-name-dropping real estate woman, it had been
a hideaway for Lex and Lana. I was never quite sure whether
she meant together or separately.

When my bride stepped over the threshold, she was welcomed by a sloshy, slumpy sound. It must have seemed that
I had signed a lease for only the pool. The carpeting was under a wall-to-wall inch of water. With the statewide block
about weather, California's building contractors have yet to
learn how to construct a watertight roof. During the winter
months the most lucrative business in Beverly Hills is roof re-
pairing. And it is a sort of cradle-to-grave profession. The way

it is practiced, the customer you had last year is the customer you'll have this and the year after.

While Dorka had a drink from the living room floor, I took Eszter on a short wade through the rest of the house. To the right was bedroom and bath, to the left a tiny kitchen. That was it. The three and a quarter rooms (there was no tub) were furnished in Early Cabana—lots of rattan, bamboo, and rice-papered walls. The tour over, Eszter stood hypnotized by a particularly odious eight-foot aquarium tank bolted to the floor under the living room window. "Who do you think loved fish that much? Lex or Lana? Don't worry, ten gallons of white paint, some of our own things, and it'll be fine. I guess. But what can you do with a built-in aquarium?" Eventually, we found the ideal use for that empty tank.

I was sure that, at that very moment, Eszter was thinking she could have found a better place to live with her eyes closed and her feet dry. But a second later the blinding rain stopped and the sun came out. At last she could see. And, in Eszter's own words, what she saw was magic.

The house nestled in a stand of proud cypress and towering eucalyptus, atop the Santa Monica Mountains, a twelve-hundred-foot range that separates Los Angeles from the San Fernando Valley. From the front windows you looked over the pool—much bigger than the house—and out across the Valley to the snow-peaked San Gabriel Mountains. During the day we could look down upon the smog in the Valley; at night on the lights of millions of people catching their breath while they watched television to see if tomorrow there would be another smog alert. Looking south lay Los Angeles. Beyond, the Pacific Ocean. Not a neighbor in sight, not even the landlord, except on the first of each month, when we always seemed to meet at the mailbox by the gate.

I had rented a room with a view and we both agreed that the pleasures and enchantment of the latter were worth the three hundred dollars a month. Nor were there any complaints from Dorka. She gloried in the discovery that the world was not one long sidewalk with an occasional tree hidden behind an iron fence. Within a week the dog was on barking, sniffing, or chasing terms with every deer, squirrel, and bird playing in the hills around us.

Someone in the family, other than I, proposed and promptly seconded the idea that what Dorka really needed was a more domesticated playmate. Chasing rabbits and teasing lizards was all very well; but when it came down to having a serious conversation about the peculiarities of human beings, whom did she have that didn't run away?

The chosen companion was a myna bird. He arrived from the pet shop announcing, "My name is Spike, my name is Spike." The next phrase he learned was one Eszter used only when the Dane truly misbehaved: "Shame Dorka, shame Dorka." Naturally, this brought a sudden end to Eszter's dream of tête-à-tête chats between the two. Or so I thought. Following the basic female concept that tit for tat is the great equalizer, Spike's speech teacher drummed in two more words. About a week later, when I came home from the office, I found that a new atmosphere of domestic harmony existed between bird and dog. The myna was perched on the mantel chatting away. Dorka, ears at attention and head cocked, loved every word of the lengthened monologue: "My name is Spike. Shame Dorka. Shame Spike."

With such success, there was no stopping Eszter. Next came "Vhere's Bruce?," a rather silly question in a house that size. But a more sensible announcement soon coincided with my nightly return from Universal: "Martini time, martini time." I am sure Spike would have gone on to even greater linguistic heights had he not outsmarted himself. Outsmarted me, would be more accurate.

It was about this time in Spike's education that I decided to explore another part of the good life, the geographical one proving so successful. Since childhood, I had been deafened by otosclerosis. The word, translated into patient language, means the anvil and the hammer have turned to bone and the one refuses to hit the other in the face of a sound wave. With a hearing aid, I heard as much as, if not more than, I wanted;

but the instrument—in those days men wore the receiver in their shirt pocket with a cord running to the earspeaker—was an annoying bore. When young and about to kiss my first girl, the contraption made a ringing noise which set back my sex education another few years. During my oral examinations at Harvard, the batteries went dead. Had Scott and Zelda Fitzgerald gone wading in the fountain of the Plaza Hotel ten years later than they did, they would have stubbed their toes on one of my hearing aids. It had fallen from my hand, one memorable New Year's Eve, during a debate about whether goldfish talked. Finally, unless you are a kangaroo, there is no place to stow all that electronic gear when making love.

I had had four operations in New York, but I was still saying "What?" A close friend, tired of the refrain, told me about a Dr. Goodhill in Los Angeles who had developed a new operative technique to cure otosclerosis. If for no other reason than the preservation of Eszter's larynx, another try was called for. The operation was a glorious success. For the first time in some thirty-odd years the sound of rain on the roof was more than just the lyrics to a pop tune of the thirties.

It was during the weeks of convalescence that the myna bird and I had it out. My ear was packed with cotton and until the swollen tissues shrunk I wouldn't know for sure if this fifth try at surgery had worked. Nevertheless, even in these early stages of the healing process a new sound occasionally would break through the barrier. Optimism was the keynote around the pool, where Eszter had deck-chaired me in the sun. Dorka knew that something nice was happening and every so often would leave her systematic digging in the bushes to lick my head bandage. (A former tenant had been the obtuse angle in a love-triangle shooting and the gun was rumored to have been hidden on the grounds. The police gave up searching for it years back. Dorka was still on the trail.) And because she thought it would be a diversion, Eszter brought out the myna bird and placed its cage on a nearby table. With Eszter present, Spike ran through his litany in full voice. However, as soon as she returned to the house or went off shopping, a nerve-shattering, incredible performance took place. Spike opened and closed his beak as in speech; yet there was total silence. My first instinct was to tell Eszter of this pantomime and she could decide if I had had too much sun. My second thought canceled the first: the operation had been a failure and those bursts of beautiful noise had given way to a permanent period of nothingness. If that was the case, I didn't want Eszter to know until the doctor's vote was in.

Several nights later I had a nightmare in which a hundred or so of Spike's sisters and brothers circled me in a geodesic cage. In chorus they were all silently mouthing, "You're deaf, you're deaf, you're deaf." I woke up, my face covered with thirty-year-old tears. Eszter got out the brandy and then the story out of me.

The following morning, according to plan, Eszter settled me on the pool deck with Spike and then announced for all to hear that she was going off to shop in Beverly Hills. After starting the car, she crept back to spy on us through the hedge which shielded the pool from wind and errant Peeping Toms. I had not been hallucinating. Eszter caught Spike halfway through his silent serenade. She stormed to the poolside, picked up his cage, and marched into the house. Later, she swore that as the two of them got closer to the house, Spike's voice became correspondingly more audible.

Early the next morning, before I was awake and could argue, Eszter returned "Spite," as he was rechristened *in absentia,* to the pet shop. It is now ten years later and my hearing is greatly improved, but we still miss and love that myna bird. To rationalize my guilt over Spite's losing out in the battle of animal fun versus human vanity, I keep telling myself it's not fair to cage a bird.

It doesn't help.

Like steak tartare or yogurt, California is not something you gulp down at first serving. The taste must be acquired, particularly by New Yorkers. So different from life anywhere else, the temptation is to compare it with the familiar flavors of back home and find the California fare wanting. Initially, for some it is too rich, for others too dull. As for ourselves, we had no trouble adjusting to the sheer physical ease of living and working in Los Angeles: to the baking sun now that it was shining on a day-in, day-out schedule, to the fresh cracked crabs, to the artichokes the size of a softball, and to the giant strawberries selling for twenty cents a box.

But there was a portion of the new life which we hated. We loathed the lack of intellectual stimulus, the depressing absence of any ideas, conversation, or humor not related to the movie or television business. We hunted in vain for a set of values, for a culture, for a morality that was not dictated by studio heads, overnight stars, and gossip columnists.

Perhaps going West had been a great mistake. Maybe we weren't young enough to qualify for Horace Greeley's dictum. One thing was certain, though: we erred by settling in the "movie colony," a community which in 1960 was following the cliquish behavior of the 1860 English Colonists as they struggled with the White Man's Burden. Hollywood's burden was the encroachment of good taste. But as the coal miner said to the lung specialist, "That's where I earn my living."

Feeling this way, we undertook the first of several trips back East to explore the possibilities of resettling there. While I scouted for a position at the networks or in publishing—I had been a magazine editor before crossing Madison Avenue from *Esquire* to CBS—Eszter would look for a house in the country. Our six months in California had made us converts: never again would we live in a prison atop an elevator shaft.

The first reconnaissance mission took place during a vacation from Hubbell Robinson Productions. Dorka was driven to a ranch in the Valley that catered to the big dogs regular kennels couldn't, or wouldn't, accommodate. We felt like parents taking Junior off to Camp Indian Name for the first time. After delivering her best there's-no-silver-cord-on-me speech and assuring the ranch owners that we knew the Dane would be given better food and care than it got at home, Eszter came up with what was really on her mind. Dorka had been so used to human companionship, would it be possible for Mr. and Mrs. Clark to let her in their house at night? We had brought her pad with us and any little corner of the house would do. Mrs. Clark said, *"NO."* All her charges were treated equally and she and her husband never had, never could, and never would dream of sharing their lodgings with one of the boarders. She ended her speech with a sixteenth-century proverb: "Who sleepeth with dogs shall rise with fleas." We drove home in silence, neither wanting to distress the other with misgivings.

Our parental qualms had been a total waste. On the return trip to pick her up, we learned that Dorka had destroyed the Clarks's forty-odd years of holding the line between man and dog. After being in residence only twenty-four hours the Dane had conned her way into their hearts *and their bed.* They very proudly showed us Polaroid shots of Dorka sleeping between them. On saying goodbye, the Clarks expressed the hope that we'd be going away again, very soon. "And when you do, Dorka must come back as our first nonpaying guest." Not a word about fleas. All in all, the Dane's vacation was a far greater success than ours.

We arrived in New York glowing with expectation and a California tan. At the end of the two weeks, both had faded to the color of silly putty. In our airtight, air-conditioned hotel room, a layer of soot coated the "Sterilized Just For You" bathroom glass. For those who wonder how so much dirt and grime manages to get into New York's hermetically sealed rooms and apartments, the explanation is quite simple. After a day on the town, everybody brings home a harvest of gunk in his or her lungs and then proceeds to cough it around the premises.

Taxi drivers no longer offered unsolicited advice on how the Dodgers or the Giants could cop the Series; now their spiel was about those "dirty niggers," those "dirty cops," and those "dirty Jews" down at City Hall. (I use the word "dirty" to clean up the conversation.) Possibly it had been the same six months earlier, but then I always switched off the cabbie's first word by turning a knob on my hearing aid. Now the only defense against these regurgitations was to get out and walk. No great sacrifice, since it had become the fastest means of travel in New York, aside from an ambulance. And if you failed to tip that cab driver you had walked out on, you would be riding in one. On second thought, maybe subways were quicker unless you count the time spent identifying muggers at police headquarters.

As for the excitement and mental stimulus we had missed so much, I finally realized that the exhilaration of Big Town was really just a euphoric frenzy at victory over frustration. Getting someone on the phone, an empty cab, a table for lunch, a baked potato without chives and sour cream, an apartment you could afford, a secretary who spells your name correctly—these are the adrenaline-pumping triumphs that let New Yorkers feel they make the world go round.

For me New York revisited was like seeing an old girl friend ten years after the fact. The bedroom eyes were filled with boredom, the flawless skin now slightly dusty. The excitement was gone. Eszter shared my reaction, if not the frame of reference.

The one thing which had not changed with time, the one happy constant, was our friends. We laughed and fought together as though Eszter and I had been away for only a long weekend. Donald was back in analysis; Xanti was doing his new painting by smearing his car tires with paint and driving back and forth across canvas laid out in the middle of Washington Square; Carol was writing another novel about her unhappy marriage; and Frank was predicting the end of the magazine industry. No one had changed. But their conversation had.

There was more and more talk, among these loyal New Yorkers, about getting away from their angry, violent city. Babs Huevelle summed it up for them all: "The day's not far off when I'll be calling Burns or Pinkerton for a baby sitter." They were becoming expatriates in spirit if not in fact. When we said our goodbyes there were little jokes about didn't we need someone to carry our bags or clean the pool.

We headed back to California almost convinced that West was best. Two more comparison-shopping trips to New York did away with the "almost."

As though to punish us for our transience, in our absence a disaster had occurred on our lovely Santa Monica Mountains. Once again we arrived under a sky black with clouds. This time, it wasn't rain. Smoke and ash choked the air. In the past twenty-four hours, thousands and thousands of acres and dozens and dozens of homes had been consumed by a brush fire. In the years ahead we were to know the fear and helplessness of facing these annual holocausts, inevitable as the sand-dry Santa Ana winds and the cigarette-smoking motorists racing through the canyons. This time it was to be only a warning. The fire had been stopped within fifty feet of our house. We found terrified deer and raccoons drinking from the ashy waters of the pool.

Our first act of commitment to California was to breed Dorka; the second, to hunt for a permanent home. They were carried on simultaneously so that there would be enlarged quarters for the expected population jump. Also, our lease stated in underlined legalese that only one dog was permitted on the premises. It turned out to be easier to find a husband for the Dane than a house for ourselves.

Eszter wanted to be absolutely certain that Dorka had at least one black puppy. I first heard about this elusive dream dog during our courtship, when I had asked Eszter if she missed Hungary.

"I often think about the sights and smells of our summer place. It was about two hours from Budapest. The scent of just-baked bread and fresh-jurned butter when we woke up each morning. My sisters and I hiding under the gooseberry and currant bushes and stuffing ourselves with berries while we talked about that summer's crop of new boys and fought over who was to get who. My father showing me how to graft fruit trees and roll your own cigarette. The wine harvest. And, of course, the first time I saw a Great Dane.

"I was about eight and walking home from the nearest village, when a pair of jet-black, magnificent Danes came galloping out of the gates of a walled estate. I just loved them and saw to it that they followed me for several miles until we reached home. I told my father I'd found them and begged to be able to keep these two unfortunate, homeless dogs. He looked at their engraved silver collars and called upon our neighbor to apologize. In tears I asked why I couldn't have a black Dane of my own and was reminded that our grandfather—our very rich grandfather—raised champion pulis. The patriarch's feelings would be hurt if I favored a 'foreign' breed, especially German."

A breeder, for whom the American Kennel Club subsequently issued an all-points bulletin, told us that the best way to get a true black was to breed a harlequin with a Canadian Blue Dane. He just happened to have the best blue stud in the West. Fifty dollars would consummate the marriage. Did we want to be present at the ceremony? Were I to compile a list of things I most wanted not to do, watching two Great Danes in the throes of intercourse would come pretty close to the top of the list. Eszter couldn't wait.

The day of the wedding, madame voyeur took two five-grain Librium, put three more capsules in the glove compartment, and with the bride-to-be sitting beside her on the front seat, headed off for the breeder's kennel in Downey, an eyesore forty miles away which has got to be the used-car capital of the world.

I was home when the two returned that evening. Dorka was sulking in the back seat. Eszter patted her head and whispered words of consolation:

"Well, that's the way men are sometimes. It's really all my fault. I should have known anyone who lived in Downey couldn't be a gentleman. But honest, Dorka, gentlemen can be bore after a while. Come on, we'll go have dinner and after a good night's sleep you'll feel different about the whole thing. Tomorrow, close your eyes and think of the babies."

I asked, "What happened?"

"She's still a virgin. That blue brute came into the bridal chamber like a soldier on furlough. No by-your-leave, no small talk, not even a little preliminary noossling. Well, Dorka's not that kind of a girl. She sat down and stayed sat for one whole hour. While I pulled her by the collar, the breeder tried to jack up the other end. Nothing doing. You sure you don't want to take her out there tomorrow?"

Silence.

"I don't blame you. It's like being an accessory to rape."

The following day they set forth again. Dorka, sensing she was booked for a return performance, gave me one of those "I'll never see you again, goodbye" looks. Eszter, who had doubled her previous day's dose of Librium, lowered the car window and shouted, "You're just like a Hungarian male! Horrible!" While the car was backing out the drive, I called, "What if we had a daughter?" Slamming on the brakes, displacing several yards of gravel, Eszter yelled back, "No daughter of mine would need this kind of help, you arrogant American!"

There is nothing like a family fight to take your mind off the terrors of freeway driving. When the two girls returned from purgatory, Eszter recounted how my parting remark that morning had started her thinking about the various weddings she had been to. She realized that they all had one thing in common besides a bride and groom—champagne or a toast of some other sort. That being the case, a great many of her women friends must have entered the bridal chamber pleasantly loaded. "Maybe that's why the groom is always carrying the bride over the threshold?" Having divined the elixir of connubial bliss, Eszter pulled off the freeway and shared her tranquilizers with Dorka. "They worked like magic. Dorka was absolutely shameless."

With Dorka's domestic problems solved, it was time we turned to ours. The period between dalliance and baby Danes is sixty-three days. If we didn't find a house in that time, our lawyer said what all lawyers say: "I won't take the responsibility." Were Dorka to have just one pup—highly unlikely— the landlord had every legal right to put us out. And he would. He was already talking about having been offered fifty dollars more a month by a "very sweet gentleman who only keeps a canary."

2

Trees and Pups and Escrow Fees

We didn't know it then, but peering through the inflationary bubbles of 1972, 1960 was a vintage year for California home buyers. Mortgage rates were under 6 per cent and the newspapers were crammed with ads offering some very nice this or thats for "No Money Down and Twenty-five Years to Pay." Of course the last time California gave away something for nothing was at Sutter's Mill in 1848. What those "For Sale" notices failed to mention was that real estate prices in and around Los Angeles were, and are, two to three times their East Coast equivalent. But as Eszter pointed out, "We promised one another to quit comparing things to New York. Anyway, if we don't live twenty-five years, the house won't cost as much."

That settled, we went about making a list of what we most wanted in a home of our own. Our musts—Privacy, Nature, and a View—made it pretty clear that the house itself was secondary. What we were really after was a mountaintop

oasis where there were no neighbors close enough to hear if
we had an echoing fight, to see when we bathed nude in the
pool, and to know if we raised all those animals esteemed for
their manure. There were house-free hilltops like that along
Mulholland Drive, but after buying the land we would not
have had the money to put up a Hooverville shack. So, we
were going to find the land and to hell with the house that
was cluttering it up. Also, we both knew that whatever home
we ended up with would be Eszter's first redesign assignment
in California.

They may not know how to make them leakproof, but
California architects have built every style dwelling from
Noah to Neutra. A television writer I knew in New York was
having monumental problems trying to get his wife to make
up her mind what period architecture she wanted for the
house they planned to build in Connecticut. While on an assignment in Hollywood, he took his Rolleiflex and walked
down the main drive of Beverly Hills, taking pictures of the
homes along the way. When the film was developed back
East, he had the following choices for his wife:

Cape Cod Salt Box	Pennsylvania Dutch
English Gothic	Frank Lloyd Wright
Swiss Chalet	"Tara"
French Provincial	Hacienda
Boston Federal	Mediterranean
English Tudor	Greek Revival
Early Colonial	Japanese Pagoda
New Orleans Rococo	Charles Addams
Western Ranch	American Gothic

The wife threw away all the photographs, except one, and
bought an old New England barn, which was reassembled
stall by stall on their property. The picture she saved, and
framed in a fake gold-and-diamond affair, shows a beautiful
old Spanish house, its perfect proportions gone slightly askew.
A huge picture window had recently been built into one of the
lovely white stucco walls fronting the street. Behind the glass

was the garage. The window framed the owner's $32,000 Rolls-Royce Silver Cloud limousine for all to admire.

Beverly Hills was not for us. We had only *a* Ford, and a one-car family, in pre-Reagan days, qualified for Welfare. Even if we painted a few Cadillacs and Jags on the inside of our garage window, "the flats," as the main residential area is called, played havoc with all three of our territorial imperatives.

PRIVACY means only one thing in Beverly Hills—what one person has that another party feels free to violate. As for NA-TURE, it is of the instant variety. Lawns are dug up and fresh ones rolled down at the first rumor of crab grass. As soon as one type of flower starts to wilt, nursery crews swarm in and plant new varieties *in full bloom*. A tulip bed becomes a petunia garden overnight, which probably explains why most Beverly Hills children fail their botany courses. And the excellence of a VIEW on the flats is judged by how many of your neighbors' rooms you can see into without the use of binoculars. To protect this inalienable right of sublimation, Section 10-3.2605 of the Beverly Hills Building Code states that no hedge or wall in the front of your property may be higher than three feet. So, saying a fond farewell to Beverly Hills, we confined our search to the hills and mountains which lie to the north. We looked at sixty-eight houses.

Buying a home is like window shopping: you spend the most time ogling what you can't afford. There was a spectacular Spanish affair on a summit overlooking the Pacific. It had a bowling alley in the cellar, a drive-in fireplace and four maids' rooms over the garage. It was advertised as a steal at $129,500. And it was, if you happened to be a master plumber who could install all new piping in and under two-foot adobe walls, woodcutting was your hobby, and you were the master of four indentured servants. With the same bravado, we dropped by a movie star's tax write-off, another one that had Catalina Island for breakfast viewing and the sun setting behind Hawaii for cocktails. The house itself teetered on the edge of a cliff, four hundred feet above the ocean. A swim-

ming pool and tennis court were cantilevered out over the
water. The tennis ball flotsam on the beach below had put
more than one industrious boy through college.

Kicking the retreads on our Ford to emphasize my point,
I asked the real estate woman why she was showing us this
house, which the actor must have built upon being turned
down for the role of Hearst in *Citizen Kane*. After a disapprov-
ing look, she said, "Oh, I know you have a budget, Mr. Colen,
but it's always wise to keep an open mind in these things. You
never know." The woman whispered those last three words
with the cunning of a gypsy fortuneteller. Eszter felt the same
lucky vibrations. We couldn't wait to get home to search our
mailbox for that legal-looking letter which would inform us
that a distant relative or, more likely, a little old woman who
had never forgotten how we stopped and helped change her
tire, had died and left us five thousand shares of IBM. Instead,
among the bills, we found a notice from the local Blue Chip
redemption center saying that the last batch of coupon books
we had turned in for a bottle warmer, part of Dorka's layette,
was short two pages of stamps.

In a community famous for its types, the genus real estate
woman has never received the attention it deserves. A strange
oversight, for in Beverly Hills the profession is almost as popular as interior decorating and demonstrating water beds.
These purveyors of the "Divorce Sale," the "Dramatic Con-
temporary," the "Tropical Paradise"—as the real estate ads are
headed—come in two types: the young and the old. The
former are actresses temporarily out of work; the latter, actresses permanently unemployed and/or women whose last
divorce netted no community property. They all drive Cadillacs, baby-blue convertibles for the ones still making casting
calls, black and hard-topped for the permanent-wave set.
Their uniform also varies with age, hot pants and minis versus
suits and hats.

The badge of the profession is a nine-by-seven-inch loose-
leaf binder containing the listings of all houses currently for
rent or sale. The ladies never let these little black books out

of their grasp and when they consult them it is with the secretiveness of a poker player holding a royal flush. For alongside each listing the agent has scribbled in code what she knows and you must not: the state of the plumbing, the termite population, the number of times the house has been burgled, the location of the cesspool, the party-throwing habits of the neighbors, and whether the property is in a flood, slide, or fire area. Whenever we were indiscreet enough to inquire about the age of the roof or the source of the pungent odor, the agent would sneak behind the covers of her bible and pop back out with a diverting anecdote concerning the sexual peccadilloes of the former tenant or how late one night John Barrymore had slept here thinking it was his own house.

These unsung heroines of the Los Angeles land boom deserve something more than their 6 per cent sales commission. Perhaps a statue in Will Rogers Park at the corner of Beverly Drive and Sunset Boulevard? Miniskirted agent standing proud among the birds-of-paradise, little black book clasped in one hand, car keys in the other. After all, were it not for their friendly persuasion, could the Beverly Hills Realty Board boast that the homes in that community change ownership on the average of every four years?

While we worked our way through several black books, tapping walls here and turning faucets there, Dorka lounged at home smugly enjoying the indulgencies of coming motherhood. Another three books of Blue Chip stamps were spent on a foam rubber beach pad which Eszter rolled out for the Dane under her favorite napping tree. Where once the dog spent nights sleeping at the foot of our king-size bed—one of Hollywood's few civilized inventions—she now slept *on* the foot, with the rolled-back spread for a cover.

Like many pregnant women, Dorka developed exotic taste buds. Kibble and horsemeat were all very well for openers, but it was raspberries and cracked crab that really turned her on. We discovered these cravings the hard way and were soon warning our Sunday outdoor luncheon guests of a new house rule: Never turn your back on a pregnant Dane.

Dorka's passion for the Good Life, stolen or handed down, was beginning to show. Either she had put on weight or the black and white spots on her belly were growing mysteriously in size. Eszter took the incipient bulge very personally.

"Ve have a saying, 'A fat dog has a fatheaded mistress.'"

I asked, "Who's ve?"

"Ve's me."

Short of installing a treadmill on the pool deck, there really was no way to give Dorka the extensive workout a 150-pound mother-to-be required. Running her up and down the driveway or around the property was out. At the first sight of Dorka's pouch, the landlord would draw up eviction papers. If we took her for walks along Coldwater Canyon or Mulholland Drive, one of two things was bound to happen. First, we would be arrested for loitering. Beverly Hills police are notoriously suspicious of anyone found outside the confines of a car. Or, secondly, we would be run over by passing motorists, since the same police have proclaimed open season on all pedestrians. I had just about settled for making Dorka swim a hundred laps of the pool when Eszter discovered a rarely used—except by fire trucks fighting hillside flare-ups—dirt road that curved its way from Mulholland Drive through brush and scrub oaks, down to the back door of Beverly Hills. From then on it was a revival of *The Champ,* that scene where Jackie Cooper takes Wallace Beery for his morning roadwork prior to the Big Fight. The only difference being that our workouts took place each evening on my return from the studio.

The three of us drove over to the start of the back road. Dorka was let out and the top of the convertible was put down. While Eszter drove at a steady ten miles an hour, I knelt in the back seat shouting all kinds of razzle-dazzle so that Dorka would keep pace with the car. She loved it, unlike poor hung-over Beery. Here was a family playing together and Dorka was jogging her damnedest to keep it together. We did four miles of roadwork each evening with periodic stops while the trainers opened a thermos of cocktails and

Dorka had a few no-cal Milkbones. The Champ got down to fighting trim; we gained a few pounds.

The count was now up to sixty-eight houses seen and rejected. This negative vote wasn't quite unanimous, because, early in our campaign, we had driven by a place which Eszter thought might have "great possibilities." For what, I didn't know, unless she had a slum renewal project in mind. But we were getting panicky and I was coaxed into going back for a closer appraisal. Even the real estate woman acted as though we were just paying a courtesy call and left her car motor running during the tour.

Violating Webster's definition, here was a dungeon above ground. At eleven o'clock in the morning you could see the fluorescent night switches glowing in the cell-like rooms. As we stumbled out the front door into daylight, Eszter looked around and asked, "How much?"

After taking a moment to recover, our guide opened her little black book and, thumbing through the pages, answered, "It's been so long since I've had an inquiry I'll have to look it up. Yes, here it is. The owner's asking sixty-five thousand, but I'm sure he'd come down."

"We couldn't stoop that low, could we, Eszter?" I said, proud of my joke and waiting for laughter. Miss Black Book giggled. Eszter was silent, lost in her evaluation of the property.

The nearly two acres were pie-shaped. The small-bite part contained a Sing Sing-size electric gate (which didn't work) and a long rock pile that was once a stone wall. Along the back property line a row of pine trees stood between the house and a field and Mulholland Drive up above. The east boundary was guarded by a phalanx of eucalyptus trees at least 200 feet high. They seemed even taller, for just in front of them ran a forty-foot-deep wash which carried the seasonal rains down into the Valley. This $65,000 serving of blue sky pie was cut into two diet-size portions by a blacktop driveway, crisscrossed with crevices, the like of which had not been seen since the San Francisco earthquake. To one side of this obstacle course lay a field verdant with weeds; to the other, a forty-five-foot swimming pool, empty except for a knee-high gumbo of black algae and rotten leaves.

I was standing on the driveway, debating which hole to jump in if Eszter decided she liked the place, when the subject of my anxiety asked, "Isn't that the most beautiful California live oak you've ever seen?" Eszter was pointing to a three-hundred-year-old giant that had staked out squatter's rights in front of the house. The tree's huge limbs threw a green awning over much of the roof.

The real estate agent, quick to grab a plus in a morass of minuses, spoke up. "It certainly is, Mrs. Colen. It certainly is. In all my years selling houses, I've never had the privilege of offering an older or more beautiful live California oak. Mrs. Colen, you really are a rare judge of—"

I cut off this idiocy. "Please, Eszter, let's get out of here. *Now.*"

"But it has the three musts: P., N., V.," she insisted.

Put that way, Privacy, Nature, and a View sounded like a venereal disease. I was getting angry and headed for the car. "It's got SOS, that's what. This place is a disaster area. How can you, a designer famous for her sunny colors, even think of living in this cellar? Planning to raise mushrooms?"

If I have not already mentioned it, stubbornness is the cornerstone of Hungarian womanhood. Eszter followed me to the car, but she wasn't giving up. "For somevun who's supposed to be creative, you have as much imagination as a soft-boiled egg. No vunder television is in such bad shape. Ve open up the house and let in the sun. That's vut ve do."

Short of dynamiting, I could not see how that might be accomplished. We drove home in silence.

For the first time since either of us could remember, Dorka was not standing at her official greeting station on the pool deck. We called. No Dorka. Eszter went to look for her inside and I searched around the back of the house. There she was, bulldozing a hole in a secluded clump of ivy. The Dane looked up just long enough for me to pat her mud-encrusted muzzle and then went back to digging. This was no common, bone-hiding hole. It was shallow and circular, and about five feet in diameter. Dorka was making her nest, a maternal chore which the vet had warned us was one of the first signs that labor would soon begin. In my firmest, most loving voice I asked Dorka to please take it easy. She might be ready, but we certainly were not.

While Eszter bathed Dorka in praise and whispered girl-talk, I headed for the phone. I got our veterinarian, Dr. Sprowl, out of surgery to find out how many puppies Great Danes usually have.

Answer: "On the average, six to eight. Good luck, Mr. Colen."

Next, I got our lawyer out of court, told him the lease was about to be violated six to eight times, and asked for his advice.

Answer: "I guess it's too late for an abortion, so if I were you I would start packing. Find a house yet? Remember what I said about not taking the responsibility."

The final call was to Miss Springer, the real estate lady of last record. When I told her why I was calling, a few minutes lapsed until she came out of shock.

Answer: "The owner is in Pennsylvania. I'll call him right away, Mr. Colen. But he's not going to be very happy about coming down to forty-five thousand from sixty-five. Are you sure you won't go a little higher?" She correctly interpreted my silence. "All right," she said, almost in tears over the twelve hundred dollars she would be losing in commission were the owner to say yes to my offer, "I'll try. After all, I guess he can't shoot me over the phone. But even if the poor man says okay, remember you can't move in until escrow is closed. That takes at least six weeks."

Escrow is a wonderful California law which insists that a third party hold the money so that neither buyer nor seller can welsh on their deal. It prevents the latter from absconding to South America with your down payment before signing over the deed or before you can find out if he really owns the place; and it discourages Mr. Buyer from reneging on his offer to purchase just because Mrs. Buyer decides, at the last moment, that numerologywise the house's street number will mess up her future. Those millions of Californians who move each year do not say, "We've bought a new home"; they announce, "We're in escrow." The first few times Eszter heard the expression, she kept looking for the salad garden. She hears with an accent, too.

Eszter had no difficulty, though, understanding my muttered confession of having made an offer for the mushroom cave. She asked, "Vot made you change your mind?"

"Necessity."

"And vot else?"

When at a loss for words, there is nothing better than a good quotation to fill the gap. I came up with Emerson's "A foolish consistency is the hobgoblin of little minds."

"Didn't you like anything?"

"The oak tree is pretty big."

Eszter left it at that, except for a promise that I would never regret having changed my mind. It was not an idle pledge. So far she has clocked about 35,040 woman-hours to keep her word (12 years×365 days×8 hours). Or, to put it another way, as Eszter has been known to, "Beverly Hills gardeners, and they don't know a petunia from a poppy, get six dollars an hour. So I figure you owe me about two hundred and ten thousand."

Whoever came up with the expression about dogs "dropping their litter" certainly was never present when a Great Dane gave birth. They don't drop. Too regal and ladylike to go in for instant births, they dribble, dawdle, and diddle. From first to last puppy, Dorka stretched out the miracle for thirty hours. But first things first.

According to the books, security, warmth, and privacy were what Dorka wanted most during her *accouchement*. The best way to provide all three was to construct a whelping box "at least five feet square." This was exactly the size of the wooden crate which Bekins had constructed at Hubbell's expense to bring my books out from New York. As Eszter helped me drag the box through a sliding glass door into the bedroom, the only place with five square feet of floor space, we vowed to call the first pup Hubbell.

Eszter turned the bottom of the crate into a triple-decker sandwich. First a layer of electric heating pads covered with a travelogue of hotel bath towels and topped off with a layer of the complete Sunday editions of the Los Angeles *Times* and the New York *Times*. A good ten pounds of newsprint. If nothing else, Dorka would be the best-informed mother-to-be since my college days, when a barrier-breaking Radcliffe student gave birth in the stacks of Harvard's Widener Library. So that Dorka and I could see what was going on, I drilled a hole in the top of the whelping house and hung an electric light.

On the morning of December 7—the day and month should have prepared us—Dorka entered her maternity suite with sagging carriage and a long-suffering look of resignation. She circled her quarters a couple of dozen times, scratching the bedding every inch of the way. When the help-wanted sections were thoroughly shredded and mixed with the financial and drama pages, Dorka flopped down on her side and watched us watching her. I had the uneasy feeling that she was thinking, "Just don't stand there, do something. After all, you got me into this mess."

While I was telling myself that only the menopause, poodle-owning set are silly enough to attribute human reactions to their dogs, Eszter said, "You look just like an aging roué who's gotten a sweet young thing knocked down. A watched pot never boils. Come on, we'd better get ready."

Getting ready for me meant adding a good stiff shot of vodka to my orange juice and putting on my midwife's uniform: a pair of bathing trunks. For Eszter it entailed rounding up some more purloined towels, sterilizing a pair of pinking shears, the only scissors in the house, and preparing basins of hot and cold water.

By the time we got back to the whelping house with the supplies, Dorka was busily licking a wet black bundle by her side. Hubbell had arrived and *her* mother, having already severed the umbilical cord, was now trying to free her first-born from its sac. According to the pros, this was my cue to get into the act. Often the bitch is unable to break open the sac fast enough and the pup suffocates. Also, the mother, in an attempt to keep a clean, sanitary bedchamber, will try to swallow the discarded sac, and other afterbirth. This will come back to mess up the house if not prevented. So I crawled in beside Dorka and helped. With my gentle tearing and Dorka's forceful licking, we got the puppy out and the sac into a waste container. Hubbell was handed out to Eszter, who trimmed and tied the umbilical cord and then rubbed her dry, courtesy of Conrad Hilton. Number One, looking as much like a black seal cub as a dog, was then placed in a large wicker laundry basket until Dorka was free to appreciate what she had done. Nor did we have time at the moment to coo and cluck over this pound of paws and flopping ears, for Dorka was pushing forth Number Two. In the next three hours six more checked in.

Mother and midwife were seriously sagging with all this traffic when Eszter, in the role of floor nurse, brought us a Hungarian revitalizer: Barack. This deliciously lethal apricot brandy was mixed with hot milk for Dorka and served straight to Bruce. I raised my glass in a toast to the limp lady. After all, she had dropped more than the average Dane litter and they were all what Eszter wanted: black. But instead of standing to acknowledge our praise, Dorka finished her milk punch, burped, and lay down to have the next one.

Seven hours later, when the twelfth puppy showed up, I found myself squatting in the whelping house, hot and light-headed, convinced that this conveyor belt of velvet packages would never stop. In my addled state, I began to see Dorka as a mechanical doughnut-maker, plunking out her product on a twenty-four-hour, seven-day-a-week schedule. And in this Kafkaesque daymare I was the full-time keeper of the machine, forever entangled in umbilical cords and afterbirths, never to leave my five-by-five prison.

The wellspring of this population explosion went to sleep, beating midwife and floor nurse by about ten seconds. Around midnight, Eszter nudged me awake and whispered, "Your dog is licking again." From about the ninth pup on, I had become the Dane's sole owner. Eszter had heard correctly. Dorka was unveiling Number Thirteen. It seemed unfair to go back to sleep leaving her alone to nurse and clean a baker's dozen, so we stayed by her side and helped as best we could.

Even if the bewildered mother had had enough counter space to feed her young, her supply of milk would have lasted only several rounds in this heavy-drinking crowd. To keep everybody happy, Eszter set up an auxiliary bar where those who were tired of standing in line, being pushed and shoved, could have a peaceful, nippled bottle of heated goat's milk. When the sun came up, the crowd was back in its basket sleeping it off and Dorka was back in labor. After the birth of Dawn—a doubly fitting name since Dorka had produced a child the color of burnt sienna—we waited six hours, hoping there would be no more eruptions. There were not. The gusher had been capped.

Following lunch, our first square meal in twenty-four hours, Dorka seemed restless. I walked her down to the foot of the driveway. After relieving herself, she tried to sit down, but I kept urging her up with a pep talk about exercise being the best thing for women who had just given birth. Her response to this bit of unsolicited medical advice was to trot off to a clump of grass, where she deposited her fifteenth child, the largest and blackest of the blacks. Replying to my panicky shouts, Eszter met us at the front door, scissors and towel in hand. She took one look and said, "That's the one *I* want. That's the one we keep. How do you call the moor in Shakespeare?"

With more than a pound of squirming, slippery newborn in my arms, I was in no condition to play Information Please and offered the first name that came to mind—Iago.

Eszter put out her hands to take him. "Welcome to life, Iago. You're going to make ours more beautiful."

Over the years, when our more literate guests have asked, "Why not Othello?," Eszter has covered me by answering, "Why not Iago? It's a nice name. Stop thinking black and white. You a racist or something?"

At two and four that afternoon, Dorka had her sixteenth and seventeenth puppy. Dorka may have known that that was it, but I didn't and I was back in the doughnut factory. What was needed just then was a call to our family doctor, requesting that he have me committed; instead, Eszter left the room to telephone the vet. Why she did not use the bedroom extension I'll never know, but there is the very definite possibility that she wished to avoid having Dorka hear we were concerned about her.

Eszter came back looking, to use one of her favorite expressions, like the mouse who had swallowed the cat. "Dorka, you did it. You can relax now. As far as Dr. Sprowl knows, there has never been a Great Dane who had so many live and healthy children." It was an honor, like the Purple Heart, which Dorka looked as though she could have done without.

Now that the assembly line was shut down, we had time to sort the litter. It was an odd lot in every sense of the word: two blue Danes the tint of an old gray fedora; four more copper-hued ones like Dawn, a beautiful color which the American Kennel Club, in all its stodgy wisdom, refuses to recognize; and eleven blacks. With Iago having that many look-alike brothers and sisters, Eszter was not taking any chances on giving away the wrong one. She painted the nails on Iago's front paws with red polish. Hubbell and Dawn had already lost their identity among the pile of brothers and sisters tumbling over, under, and around each other.

Short of sewing on name tags, we gave up the idea of trying to christen each one. The puppies would have to struggle along without benefit of baptism. Our method of identification was a moment-to-moment thing, a study in existentialism, i.e., "Hand me the one with pablum in his eye," "The guy with his tail in his mouth gets the bottle next," or "The blue peeing under the coffee table wasn't bathed yet." The exception to this no-name rule were the two male and two female copper-colored ones. They were each called Mrs. Brown.

Ma Barker's deceptions in hiding her murderous clan were nothing alongside our ploys to keep the landlord from discovering what we had stashed away. It began to look as though being in escrow was to be a permanent way of life. The owner of what we thought would be our new home had left the country, leaving his property so encumbered with debts, his own lawyer gave up trying to untangle the liens. When finally we moved into this debtor's castle, I discovered the garage floor covered with an inch-thick layer of unpaid bills and dunning letters. Among them was a $1,682.15 invoice from Schwab's Drug Store in Beverly Hills. Eszter, looking over my shoulder, said, "That poor, sick man." Before she went on to suggest that out of sympathy we raise our offering price for the house, I reminded her that, in California, druggists sell liquor as well as sleeping pills.

So, while our attorney took on the long and arduous task of settling the owner's debts (after all the bills and mortgages were paid, he realized about four hundred dollars in cash), we played hide-and-seek to stave off eviction. When the landlord asked why all the front windows of the house were covered with sheets, we claimed that the sun was starting to fade the rug. Actually, the hideous aquarium defacing the picture window had been converted into an ideal puppy run. When Dorka was taken for a walk, we both had to go along. One to hold the leash, the other to walk nonchalantly beside her, hiding those telltale undulating bosoms. The milkman was instructed not to leave the six quarts of goat's milk by the entrance to the pool house but to hide them under an oleander bush. When the litter was old enough for outdoor sports, a baby's play pen was hidden behind the house and I smuggled the puppies to Eszter through a back window. Toward the end of our tenancy, the whelping house became known as the yelping house. To counter these choruses of yaps, we played Bach on the turned-up hi-fi from morning to bedtime.

The irony of all of this subterfuge was that when we were finally *out* of escrow and fifteen of the puppies had been sold or given away—Iago had a twinlike brother, Rousseau of the white nail polish, we wanted to hold on to as long as possible —the landlord, with a higher-paying tenant up his sleeve, sent us an official eviction notice for "destroying the aesthetic charm of his pool house" (bedsheets), and "for loud and raucous behavior" (Bach).

3

Camping In

Fortunately, for nostalgia's sake, I went through the carrying-the-bride-over-the-threshold routine back at the pool house, because there was no chance for this sentimental bit at our new home. There was no threshold. Coming right down to it, there was no front door. One or two other things were missing, like the side of the house which should have faced the Valley, one third of the roof, and an exterior wall in the master bedroom. Interior walls, in the center of the house, had been knocked down just as recklessly. The five tiny, cell-like rooms I had complained about were now two. When Eszter had said, "Ve open up the place and let in the light," she had meant just that. The day the place was officially ours, she mustered a crew of carpenters and, armed with crowbars and axes, they had attacked the dungeon with all the gusto of a bunch of kids kicking down sand castles.

When the cacophony of Skil saws and hammering had dropped back through the sound barrier and when the cloud of plaster dust haloing my head had finally drifted out through the open roof, I asked Eszter, "Do you mind if we sit down? I'd like to ask a few questions."

"Not at all. It's your house. You sit there. I'll take this one." With the *savoir-faire* of a hostess offering two matching Louis XV armchairs, Eszter gestured toward a pair of ancient toilet bowls which had been ripped out of the bathrooms and lay atop the mound of debris in the living room.

I started by cautioning, "Now remember, we're having a discussion, not an argument."

"So you vant to fight. You vant to spoil our first day in our beautiful new house."

"That's precisely what I don't want to do. It's just that I thought we decided we didn't have the money *to build* a new house."

"Ve don't. This is vut you Americans call remodeling."

"And vut do you call it in Hungary?"

"Building."

"Okay, drop it. Are there any plans, any blueprints, for this open-air theater?"

"Of course. I'm a professional, aren't I?"

"Where are they?"

"In my head, *dummkopf.*"

"You know I don't understand Hungarian."

"That's German, you *buta fiú.* Any more questions?"

Before the controversy was shifted to the UN, I tried a friendlier, more conciliatory approach. "In the plans that are in your head, has any area been set aside where we can sleep while Ms. Frank Lloyd Wright creates her swan song?"

"If you'd stop knawking for one moment, you'd see the maid's room hasn't been touched. That's vare ve sleep."

It was true. The wrecking ball had not ricocheted off that section of the house, a ten-by-eight bedroom with a broom-closet-size bathroom which would have thwarted even President Harding. The former owner believed in a simplistic theory of décor. Want to make a room seem bigger? Paper with something big. The maid's cell was covered with herds of mammoth black elephants, stampeding through Kelly green foliage.

Over the coming years, these quarters were to be a barometer of our fortunes. When the going was good and when some

Scandinavian friend knew of a young girl willing to work to "see California," it was a maid's room. These Nordic visitors were as permanent as the resolve of their boyfriends back home. As soon as a letter arrived via SAS saying that a divorce was in the works, or that absence had made the heart grow constant, it was goodbye Disneyland, hello Trivoli Gardens. Dishes were left in the sink and wash on the line, while I sped the young lady and her new Ohrbach trousseau to Los Angeles International Airport for the next flight to Copenhagen.

When times were normal—maidless, that is—the wing served as a guest room for friends and relatives. Eszter eventually transformed the tiny box into a surprise package, but she held back on her talents enough to preserve some of the room's claustrophobic feeling and our drop-in trade left after a few days.

Edna Ferber, that most productive author, devised three stratagems to be sure that her weekend guests in Stepney, Connecticut, left on Sunday night so she could get back to the typewriter early Monday morning.

1) Sunday at lunch, she would hand her guest some letters with the request, "The postal service is terrible up here and these are rather important. Would you mind dropping them in a mailbox when you get back to New York tonight?"

2) When guests returned to their rooms after Sunday lunch, they found that the beds had been stripped.

If neither of these ploys started a round of goodbyes before sundown, the *coup de grâce* took place.

3) A maid would arrive and, interrupting the tarrying weekender, say, "Beg your pardon, madam, but I'm just about to pack your things. What shall I leave out for the trip back to town?"

I have always thought that Miss Ferber would have applauded Eszter's deliberate lack of inspiration in redoing the guest quarters.

When the going was gone and we had to save every penny, Eszter's workshop, a tiny two-room house hidden away in a corner of the property, was enlarged and converted into a lovely revenue-producing tenant cottage and the maid's room/ guest room suddenly became a *spacious* design studio.

Now that I knew there was to be a roof over our heads while the remodeling droned on, I asked where Dorka and her two sons were to sleep. Eszter was ready with a logical reply: "If it's big enough for us, there will be plenty of room for them."

And so that night, the first of one hundred and fifty similar evenings spent camping out on the African veldt, the five of us faced 362 charging elephants. There were more, but peeling pachyderms, where pink plaster showed through, didn't count in my nightly game of totting up the herd. It was like sitting in row AA during a three-dimensional Cinerama feature. One became too dizzy to sleep. By the end of the first week, Eszter had made us each a pair of blackout eye shades from the seat of my last pair of Brooks Brothers dark-gray flannels. Cutting through my loud protests, Eszter explained, "When are you going to learn a Madison Avenue uniform is just a security blanket? Anyway, your counting keeps me awake."

The dogs had a more immediate approach to the problem. When a particular elephant bothered them, they got up and walked over to where they could bark under his trunk. Incensed that their adversary didn't backtrack, the Danes rose on their back legs and scratched off a piece of elephant hide big enough to grasp in their teeth. Each pulling a strip of paper from the wall, they returned to the rug by the bed and settled down to see who could make the smallest spitball. Given the choice of facing those 362 elephants each evening and the first thing every morning, or having a confetti factory in the center of the room, we condoned the latter.

Anyway, within a few weeks Dorka & Co. would have a playmate who managed to make them look like the neatest kids on the block.

For most people the Sunday paper means the weekly diversion of crossword puzzles, comic strips, or studying the real estate ads. For Eszter it's the pets-for-sale column. Each week she reads these listings with the concentration of an aerospace engineer scanning the help-wanted section. I could be, have been, and will be asked any of the following questions over a Sunday breakfast:

"Voodn't two vhite peacocks look vunderful down in the field?"

"You know, if ve got a goat, she'd help you clean up all the brush around the place. I'll milk her, don't vorry."

"Do you think ve could keep a monkey without caging it?"

"Vhat about a parrot? They're nothing like myna birds."

"Don't you think every true Hungarian should own a puli? No vunder Zsa Zsa has all those silly miniature poodles. I've always suspected that she vus Bulgarian."

"If ve ever have three hundred and fifty dollars to spare and you vant to get me a surprise birthday present, I'll be expecting a miniature horse. They're no bigger than Dorka."

My routine answer to these testings is either no or "Please pass the marmalade"; but on our first Sunday at home, I was still suffering from remodeling shock, a very real psychic disorder which some enterprising young psychiatrist would be wise to specialize in. Think of the referrals: architects, interior decorators, contractors. And during a depression, the doctor might leave his card on the counter of do-it-yourself emporiums. But getting back to that particular Sunday.

Through the low hum of nonexistent saws and beating hammers, the first symptom of the Remodeling Syndrome incidentally, I heard Eszter saying something about a new shipment of raccoons and wouldn't the dogs have fun playing with one? In normal times and feeling normal, I would have killed the suggestion right then with a "Please pass the marmalade." However, this was a cold, toastless breakfast. The contractor had started rewiring on Friday and left us without electricity for the weekend. Any excuse to get out of the place was welcome.

Five of us drove off to the pet shop; six came back. On the ride home, the seven-week-old raccoon draped itself, boawise, around Eszter's neck. The three Danes, lined up in the back seat, took turns nuzzling their new toy with a loving mixture of curiosity and extra gentleness. A lick of his furry coat was worth three swipes of the nose any day. The famous Brink's Robbery had just taken place in Boston. Our newest passenger on the ark had a harlequin-shaped bandit's mask guaranteed to fool the FBI. The raccoon was named Brinks.

He was cute, inquisitive, and brave. A great clown, a magnificent rogue.

I was afraid of him.

Eszter knew it, and so did Brinks. The raccoon played on my timidity; Eszter pretended it did not exist. After all, I had not as yet come out with the public declaration, "I, Bruce Colen, am terrified by Brinks," a seven-week-old pound-and-a-half ball of mischief struggling to survive, hoping not to end up as a silent observer in the cheering section of a Harvard-Yale football game. Eszter's bond of silence had something to do with the fact that she was on the scene, close by my side, when the cause of this fear raised its ugly, toothy head. To be precise, we were in bed together. I mean that "we" in the X-rated sense of the pronoun—Eszter, Bruce, and Brinks. I'll explain.

Everyone knows that raccoons are nocturnal creatures. Almost everyone. Brinks didn't. He found the daily destruction going on around him so educational that, until the house was finally completed, he gave up sleeping during the day. Not until the workmen quit did he hunt for a spot to rest his scheme-weary head.

Even if there had been exterior doors on the house, we could not shut him out at night. The enticing smell of his native Oregon woods was still in Brinks's memory and I am sure he would have run away looking for a tall redwood where he could spend the night in the penthouse suite. There were no doors inside, either, so we screened off the maid's bathroom with the large "For Sale" sign that had stood outside our gate. We put a kitty litter box in the bathtub, placed a towel-covered pillow on the bath mat—no need for fresh water, he

had already learned to drink from the toilet bowl—and barricaded him in for the night. First thing next morning, we
went to check if there were any complaints. No Brinks. Only
a dent showed on the pillow. The medicine chest and hamper
were empty. Searching for an explanation, I started to recall
aloud all of John Dickson Carr's locked-room mystery plots.
Eszter raised her hand. "Shuu, I hear him snoring." If you
were tired, tiny, locked in a bathroom and wanted a comfortable pad for the night, where would you sleep?

In an open Kotex box, of course.

When we stopped laughing, Eszter said, "That's no place
for a boy, Brinks," and went off to prepare more suitable accommodations in the top drawer of the one bureau we had
managed to wedge into the bedroom. Judging by his hangout
the night before, Brinks needed warmth and security, so out
went Eszter's negligees—"These are a waste in this room, anyway"—and into the top tier went a Dorka hand-me-down:
an electric heating pad, covered with a layer of absorbent
cotton. That evening Brinks was tucked in and the drawer
shut just far enough so that he might breathe but not fall out.
Several times during the night, Eszter crawled over me and
tripped over the dogs to check on the temperature of the heating pad.

I slept on the outside of the bed, since Iago and Rousseau
were not yet housebroken. They had to be taken for a 2 A.M.
walk. Their slowness in training was forgivable, our indoors
being so indistinguishable from the outdoors. When it was
rainy or cold, I leaned out of the window and placed them on
a cement walk to solve their problems unattended. There
was an old-fashioned iron radiator under the window and
one frigid night Iago tried to pull me out while I was trying
to pull him in. During the tug o' war my thigh hit that
heater. I received first-degree burns. They were nothing
compared to what the puppies got. Within forty-eight hours
they knew the house rules by heart. The 2 A.M. shift was
phased out.

Brinks was clearly a slugabed. At six-thirty, when we

dragged ourselves up—we had to have coffee ready for the workmen when they arrived at seven or about an hour's labor was lost in sulking—the raccoon was as silent as a church mouse. And just as elusive. The top drawer was empty. We were beginning to feel like motel owners whose most trusted customer skips at dawn without paying the bill.

The bedroom, crowded with packing boxes and furnished in Early Orange Crate, was harder to search than the bath had been. Eszter turned to Dorka for help. "Where's Brinks, Dorkie? Find Brinks." Dorka went over to the chest of drawers and sniffed.

"No, Dorka, he's not here. See?" And she pulled out the empty drawer, turning it upside down as though instructing a dense first-grader. "Now find Brinks." Dorka held her ground and was now pawing at the bureau. Eszter turned from teacher to a carnival pitchman playing the shell game.

"Look. Drawer Number Two." And as she turned it over, spilling the contents on the floor, "Just socks and shirts. Satisfied?" The Dane obviously wasn't and looked at Eszter with friendly condescension.

"Okay, Dorka, if that's the way you want it. Drawer Number Three. Sweaters and blouses." Now she was beginning to sound like an elevator operator at Lord & Taylor. Dorka started to whine. I can't say I blamed her.

"That's just bedding in the bottom one. I'll show you. Why can't you be like Lassie? She always finds everything." With that, Eszter turned over the final drawer and out tumbled Brinks, blankets and all. Between the back of the drawers and the rear of the chest there were about three inches of empty space which Brinks had used as a back staircase. We stuffed the egress with paper and considered the problem solved.

Act III. Same Setting. Same Day. Night: Should Eszter ever seek a divorce, I know what her first line of offense will be. "Judge, he goes to sleep at the drop of a head." This, from a near insomniac, is very damaging evidence. And if, by some misfortune, the presiding judge has trouble going to sleep himself, my case will be lost before I have a chance to tell *what she does*. Instead of pills, Eszter relies on mystery books as a sedative. With the lamp glaring, she gulps down one a night before reaching for the light switch. Merely reading the dust jacket and the dedication page makes me feel sufficiently drowsy. To add insult to injury, once asleep nothing can awaken me until the sun shines through the window. Eszter takes a perverse delight in pointing out to one and all—friends, delivery boys, storekeepers, gas station attendants (she even told a meter maid who was handing me a ticket)—that I am probably the only Californian living on the San Andreas Fault who managed to sleep through the 1971 Earthquake. Poor Eszter; if Iago's stomach rumbles from too much horsemeat, she springs awake. Given this marital disparity in sleeping habits, you can imagine Eszter's annoyance when I awoke her around midnight.

"What the hell did you put in this bed?"

"Go away! Can't you see I'm sleeping?"

"Eszter, wake up. There's something in this bed."

"Well, put it out and be quiet."

"I can't. I'm afraid."

"What is it?"

"Something hairy and sort of flat. And I think it's got one cold, wet finger."

"You just had a nightmare, that's all. Now go back to sleep, please."

"But the nightmare's moving."

"*Istenem.* Turn on the light, then. You'll feel better."

"I'm scared to move."

"Oh, for God's sakes, where is it?"

"Between my legs."

That got her up. Turning on the bedside light, Eszter found me lying on my back, still and stiff as a mummy. And twice as pale. She peeled back the covers and the red-and-white-striped "shortie" flannels I was wearing. To Eszter's credit, she held her laughter to ten seconds.

"You can look. It's only Brinks."

I slowly lifted my head a few inches, just high enough to peer over my stomach. The raccoon was sleeping between my thighs. I shivered.

"Don't worry. He won't hurt you. He was looking for some place warm."

"God Almighty, will you *please* get him out of there. He bites."

"He does not bite. He nibbles."

"I'm in no position to argue. Just put him back in the drawer and turn up the heating pad." Adding, to myself, "To roast."

I finally got back to sleep and to nightmares which only Freud would have been up to analyzing.

Three times in the next week, Brinks jimmied his way out of the bureau and brought his sleeping bag back to the same campsite. The moment I tried to move him, I received a bite-size nibble and Eszter had to airlift him out of there. She wasn't finding it funny anymore. Now, neither of us was sleeping. Something had to be done. But what? Wearing football pants to bed for the rest of my life seemed the safest solution since no hook, catch, chain, or snap affixed to the drawer was Brinks-proof. I was seriously considering nailing the drawer shut, *permanently*, when Brinks saved me from myself and himself in the bargain.

Established as a consummate escape artist, the raccoon had moved on to master thermochemistry and in the process discovered that dogs have a higher body temperature than humans. Henceforth, he slept sandwiched between the Danes. They welcomed him with open arms, offered their round bellies as king-size pillows, and vied with one another for the delight of having a floppy ear explored by his cold, wet nose. Danes are the best baby tenders in the world, contrary to the canard, undoubtedly started by some sweet old nanny sacked for pilfering silver porringers, that their size and strength are hazardous. They are far safer and far more dependable than the two-dollar-an-hour television-watching variety of baby sitter. Brinks was in good hands and out of our hair, for the time being at least. We could get back to the work of turning our no man's land into what one day *Life* magazine would call "A Beautiful House of Flowers," and *House Beautiful* "A Blithesome Blossoming World."

"We" is not the right pronoun, for I spent each day in a relatively peaceful bungalow office at Universal Studios, while Eszter contended with the questions, temperaments, and whims of: building inspectors, inspectors of building inspectors, cement truckers, plumbers, electricians, masons, carpenters, tile setters, fire inspectors, painters, and police. The last cruised by because "we wanted to see who finally bought the place. You sure got guts, lady." At least once a day, Eszter was saved from pushing her self-destruct button by Fred Vandemeer, our fatherly contractor.

This wonderful man, eyes as deep a blue as his well of honesty, was a veteran of one too many remodeling jobs. He had a fiery ulcer that needed constant milk baths. Fred and Eszter's relationship was symbiotic in the best sense of the word. They canceled out each other's anxieties. When the plumber, after eight twelve-dollar hours of poking about, couldn't find the septic tank; or after a carpenter hung a door so that it opened in when it was supposed to swing out, I could almost hear Eszter's screams five miles away at the studio. Patting the twinge in his stomach, Fred would amble over to the scene of noise pollution and deliver his standard line,

"Now, Eszter, take it easy. Rome wasn't built in a day and I got a feeling this place is going to take a little longer."

As often as she heard this corny prediction, it made Eszter laugh and head for the kitchen to fetch a glass of milk, which she handed Fred along with her own lecture:

"Now, Fred, drink down. You wouldn't need this if you'd learn to explode like me. It's so easy and healthy."

My absence from the field of battle also extended to Friday afternoons, when, after the workmen had been paid and gone home, Eszter and Fred sat down to add up how much money was left and how much work was still to be done. By the fourth Friday, it was evident that the cost of labor hung like a red cloud over our building budget and unless a miracle happened—like H.R. Productions doubling my salary—we would never be able to afford half the structural changes which were in the resident designer's head. The miracle occurred.

Hubbell fired me.

"Fired" is hardly the term to use for the gentlemanly and generous way I was treated, for under Hubbell's stern exterior was a quality which Moss Hart attributed to George S. Kaufman, a "marshmallow heart." In the grind-'em-out, grind-'em-up world of commercial television, that brand of marshmallow is for burning. Hubbell Robinson Productions was absorbed by Universal and there was only room in the sponge for Hubbell.

The two worst things about being unemployed are telling your wife and the money stopping. Which is harder to take depends upon the wife. Eszter was temporarily ecstatic. Universal's loss was her gain. She now had a full-time helper who would labor for room and board.

Is anything more touching, or subject to more revision, than the faith of a new bride? Having been married a little over a year, Eszter and I had not had enough time to confess all the big secrets of our respective pasts, let alone the little ones. Like the fact that the last time I held a hammer in my hand was when I tried to screw the can opener to the kitchen wall of my New York apartment. It wasn't so much that I didn't know how to do it as that I didn't want to do it. Being a handyman took time from more rewarding pursuits. As our home became just that, a most satisfying pleasure, and when I learned the high cost of house calls by plumber and electrician, this "let George do it" philosophy was swapped for a two-volume Home Owners' Manual. It was a quick trade, since "let Eszter do it" was clearly not the answer. Her mechanical dexterity reaches its zenith with the sharpening of a pencil and then only if an electric machine is used. Nor are labor-saving devices the answer to her mechanical block.

Just the other day we had another session on why electric can openers will not work on a tin of anchovies. With no way out, I eventually became the fastest washer-changer in the West. But at the start I chose the shovel over the saw, the rake over the rasp, and put myself out to pasture. It wasn't retirement; more a form of working exile.

Surrounding the house lay nearly two acres of chaparral, a maze of stiff-branched, low-lying shrubs, clustered in dense thickets. The early Spanish cowboys, riding through this cover, had to wear *chaparajos,* or chaps, to keep their legs from being raked bone-deep. Chaps were out. I wasn't going to make a fool of myself, clumping around like some bowlegged stand-in for John Wayne. Knee-high rubber boots and knee-length *lederhosen* made up my working outfit.

Not quite all the land was choked with chaparral. In a few comparatively open spots lurked poison oak, tumbleweed, and ankle-twisting rocks. And here and there were tiny islands of tropical vegetation. The last, halfhearted attempts by former owners to "landscape" contained the very plants we hated most: dumb cactus, phallic dangling banana palms, waxy-looking birds-of-paradise, colorless aralia, and messy acanthus. Everything had to go except two huge lacy balls of tumbleweed put aside for Christmas decorations.

Ten truckloads of brush and drab foliage rumbled out the gate on their way to the local dump. That did not include the tons of rocks and shale which I shoveled into our private disposal bin, the forty-foot gully that ran along one edge of the property. In the years ahead, those refuse trucks were to pay spring and fall visits; for there is a partnership in Southern California between God, the rubbish firms and the Department of Water and Power. The unholy alliance goes something like this: Nature sees to it that for a good part of the year there is no rain, only sun, sun, sun. From this imbalance follows the immutable law "Don't water and thou shalt perish from brush fires." But there is a reverse law, "Irrigate and thou shalt drown in greenery." Since the latter fate is preferable to the former, the only escape is to turn on the sprinklers and cut back the trees, bushes and flowers, which grow like Jack's beanstalk. Then hire a refuse firm to tote away the cuttings. There is a final guarantee that the hillside homeowner can't win. In this land which made the outdoor barbecue famous and where no self-respecting backyard would be caught without one, it is against the law to get rid of your brush the old-fashioned, inexpensive way, by burning it in an outdoor incinerator. The day cannot be far off when our twenty-five-dollar-a-load refuse collector will press our brush into logs and sell them back to us for charring steaks.

While pulling out the chaparral or digging up small rocks, I had the recurrent daydream that all my labors would end in a bonanza—black gold. At any moment an excavated root, a turned-over boulder, would reveal a trickling pool of oil. Even before I had a chance to stick my finger in the gooey mass and taste it, the puddle would erupt into a gusher, Eiffel Tower-high. If it could happen in the middle of Wilshire Boulevard, where the derrick is camouflaged behind the façade of a fake office building, why not in the privacy of Coldwater Canyon? When our well came in, I knew exactly how we were going to celebrate. The swimming pool would be filled with gin and vermouth, ten to one, and all our friends would be invited over to bob for olives. I told our lawyer of my reverie. He reacted like every other member of his profession. He turned kill-joy and suggested that I reread our deed to see who owned the mineral rights. The lovely game was over. Los Angeles County was sole heir to any gold, black or yellow, that came out of any hole on our property. On the other hand, gopher holes and their tenants were all ours.

However, there was a consolation prize in the lower field. Under a stand of wild anise lay one thousand feet of unused sprinkler pipe. Exactly what was needed to keep the place fire-retardant green. Obviously, someone else had once had the same idea, but why had he not gone ahead with the project after spending several hundred dollars for all that conduit? Various answers came to mind. Perhaps a divorce or death in the family made the preservation of the property suddenly meaningless. Or, maybe, some petty thief had used our land, deserted for so long, as a hiding place for this strange loot. Now, after eleven years of going to sleep and waking up with the same mental list of things which should be done, I think I've solved The Mystery of the Empty Pipes. That iron pile in the field was a monument to the homeowner's curse: procrastination.

All my city-born doubts about being able to handle the chores and problems of a landowner vanished the moment I had installed that sprinkler system. It was child's play. As a matter of fact, I had not had as much fun or a greater feeling of accomplishment since mastering my first Erector set. If you have the dexterity to screw a top back on a bottle, then you are halfway to being a certified pipe fitter. First you lay the pipes out, end to end, in the area you want watered. Next, one length of pipe screws into another with the aid of a coupling, sort of a large wedding band binding them together. Wherever you want a sprinkler head, a T joint is used instead of a coupling. Dig six-inch trench, lay pipe in same. Cover pipe with earth and turn on water. Presto, the fountains of Versailles on Bastille Day. It took me less than three days to make the two acres droughtproof. One small point. Do not place a sprinkler head within range of the main water valve. I got very tired of having to wear a bathing suit each time I turned the system on or off.

Apropos of absolutely nothing at all, Women's Libbers may want to avoid the pleasures of pipe fitting, for male chauvinism has extended to the jargon of the plumber's trade. The first time I entered a hardware store and asked for six elbow joints—they let the sprinkler system turn corners— the clerk sized me up and asked, "You want male or female elbows, mister?" Not having the faintest idea what he was talking about, and loath to admit my ignorance about the difference in the sexes, I asked for three of each. I felt like a first-year medical student buying a skeleton. It seems a pipe or coupling which is so threaded that it fits inside another pipe is called a male. The receiving pipe, pardon the expression, is known as a female. In defense of the P.I.P.E. of America, it must be understood that if all pipes were threaded the same way they would never get together. There must be a message in this somewhere.

With the land cleared and irrigated, it was time to start planting, if we wanted to catch the spring growing season. Eszter had been waiting for this moment all her life. There had never been enough time or the right place for her love affair with flowers to flourish. War, travel, and apartment living are not exactly the most fertile conditions for a passionate gardener.

"Passionate" is not too strong a word, for without flowers within sight and touch, Eszter would have trouble spiritually surviving. Their beauty, their courage, their innocence provide the faith and sustenance that others find in religion. Every day of our life together, there have been flowers at the bedside to say good morning. No meal, however simple or quick, is eaten without a pitcher of greenery and blooms to feed the other senses. Every room of the house, bathrooms included, are miniature flower stalls. Puddles of fallen leaves and circles of golden pollen make stepping stones across the oak floors. On New York's East Nineteenth Street, Eszter's flowering window boxes were the pride of the neighborhood. But you can have only so many windows with southern or western exposure; and besides, it is a little awkward to plant and harvest through an iron grate. Buying our first house was, in every sense of the word, Eszter's first chance to put down roots. And she made up for those gardenless years with a zeal that gladdened the hearts and jangled the cash registers of nurserymen from Los Angeles to Santa Barbara.

With the house only half-finished, the area surrounding it looked like exactly what it was—a dumping ground for broken bricks, shredded wallpaper, piles of cracked plaster and splintered wood. No chance to lay out flower beds there. So Eszter started on the areas I had cleared, each side of the driveway. She showed up for work in an outfit that would have gotten her thrown out of any gardening club and right into the nearest boxing camp. Sneakers, a two-piece sweat suit, and trimmed fingernails were the uniform of the day.

In the first month of dawn-to-dusk labor, Eszter planted nine thousand shoots of Algerian and Hahn ivy. But she had help. Brinks was her assistant. Each morning he arrived perched on Eszter's shoulder and while she dug a cavity for each slip, he spent the day burrowing nearby. Satisfied with the dimensions of a particular excavation, Brinks would scurry over and pull Eszter's hair. This was the signal for her to fill his hole with water and drop in a sugar cube from the supply in her pocket, which he promptly washed away to glucose. Today, the ivy on that slope is as fat and healthy as a "before" model for Weight Watchers. Eszter's other pocket was crammed with crackers for the kibitzing bluejays perched in nearby trees. Feeding these great teasers—they would swoop down and pluck a saltine from between her lips—broke the monotony of nine thousand plantings. Every now and then, Brinks switched to playing in the pile of manure Eszter was using to enrich the soil around each shoot. But no matter how engrossed, as soon as Brinks heard the hammers and saws stop for the lunch break, he called it quits and joined the workmen in the garage for a brown-bag buffet.

When the fellows went back to work, Brinks hung around a little longer to open and scramble about in their toolboxes. The master carpenter on the job was a meticulous craftsman who kept the contents of his work chest as clean and neat as an old maid's hope chest. His box was Brinks's favorite playground. Nails and screws of all sizes were ferreted out of their individual slots and sloshed around in a pile, over which glue was spilled. The confection was then topped off with a sprinkling of nuts, bolts, and bits of sandpaper. Steve was philosophical about the mess and spent several hours each week cleaning his tools. At seven fifty an hour, it was proof that tolerance is golden.

With the ivy planted and the trowel blisters on her hand hardened, Eszter turned to the large field down by the gate. She wanted to blanket it with white daisies and wild flowers. I wanted to turn it into a small orchard. We compromised. Between the holes I dug for orange, lemon, peach, avocado, and lime trees, Eszter wrestled and clawed with the adobe soil until it gave up and turned over, worked in yards of nitrogen-rich fertilizers and soil-breathing mulch. She then sowed her bag of seeds: Shirley, California, and Flanders poppies; feverfew, cornflowers, larkspur, black-eyed Susans, and lupine. And with childhood memories of the European countryside, wheat was sown here and there and one hundred tiny marguerites were nestled into the soil.

That wild, blooming orchard was the testing ground for Eszter, the gardener. While she had the instinct and bursting urge to make things grow, up until that moment her how-to-do-it knowledge of horticulture came from books, nursery catalogues, and that bible of Southern California gardeners, the *Sunset Western Garden Book*. Also, Eszter found that, when in doubt, there was nothing like a call to her friendly nurseryman, Jim Stevens. He genuinely loved the seedlings, bushes, and trees he sold and was anxious to share what he knew to keep his children alive. Were it not for Jim's tutelage, Eszter would have been a slow-blooming gardener.

When the field came into flower, Eszter graded herself and settled for a B —. Number One, the marguerites had grown so bushy and tall that they were killing each other fighting for a place in the sun. Only in California do these daisies grow to such proportions. When we wanted to shut up the Danes for the night, they were able to play a very successful game of hide-and-seek behind the giant white mushrooms. Seventy of the hundred marguerites had to be transplanted to other areas. No problem; barren spots we had. Number Two, Eszter found that she could not, cannot, and has given up trying to grow lupine.

"Every week, weekend gardeners from here to Mexico grow these damn beautiful things. Why can't I? God is getting even with me for not liking cactus."

His retribution extended to one other plant, which everyone else in the world can grow: chives. Her frustration over this defeat has made the herb a dirty word around the house and we settle for cut-up shallot tops in our baked potatoes. If the tops are young, it's the kind of sacrifice any gourmet will gladly make.

Up until The Planting of the Ivy—a feat worthy of capitals —Eszter and I had always thought of snails as residing on tin-lined copper saucepans bathed in garlic, butter, and herbs. The only thing you had to be careful of was not to eat them unless your dinner partner was having the same. We discovered, however, that, in California, snail eating was a two-way affair.

The size of an inflated half-dollar, our local snails hid from the midday sun in damp coverts, then slowly strolled out each evening to eat all the young, green shoots in sight. And their hundreds of brothers and sisters, aunts and uncles, parents and grandchildren joined them in the gastronomic tour. Eszter's daily ivy settings proved to be the nightly high point in their version of a progressive dinner. Snail bait would have solved the problem, but we did not know then that dogs steer clear of these arsenic-loaded pellets and we looked for another solution.

At the turn of the century, a French immigrant to California grew tired of robust western food and, longing for an aromatic serving of *escargots,* sent back to France for some live snails so that an ever-ready supply would always be on hand for the oven. They got out of hand, as does everything in California, and swept across the state at a speed well calculated to put to rest, once and for all, the expression "snail's pace." Cursing the gluttonous importer, Eszter remembered what French farmers do to keep the mollusk population under control. "Ve get ducks. They vill get the snails; you vill get the eggs."

We bought two ducks, but they were not around long enough for me to find out what was so special about the eggs. I built a small lean-to down in the field. That way, their house would be in the center of snail country. The following morning I expected to find the two birds stuffed to the bills and quacking for more after their all-night snail binge. What I found were more snails than ever and no ducks. I beat the bushes, combed the gully, and—not knowing that ducks do not roost—scanned the limbs of nearby trees. No ducks. Heading back to the house to ask Eszter how Frenchmen kept their ducks down on the farm, I walked past the pool which had just been mucked out, sandblasted, plastered, and refilled. Cruising the pristine surface of this wonderful luxury—as Easterners, we still feel a delicious, satisfying guilt when using it—were the two missing ducks. They looked like Back Bay biddies making a white-glove inspection tour of the Left Bank hotel Cooks has booked for them.

Now, I knew that ducks took to water like ducks; but after a good bath and swim, it was my understanding that they went back to dry land to sunbathe, gossip, eat, and sleep. Not these ladies. To entice them into leaving, Eszter lowered herself to the point of foraging for a dozen plump snails, which she lined up in a trail from the pool deck to the field. The ducks flopped out for as long as it took to stow away these road directions and then, splash, back they went. Taking a more forceful approach, I turned the hose on them. They loved it. I threw very large pebbles. They dove to fetch. Finally, the three Danes were called into action. No luck. As soon as they swam within range, the sitting ducks turned into flapping, off-white windmills and the dogs flew out of the pool. This went on for several days. While the snail population skyrocketed, the ducks piddled their lives away. The pool turned green, although the chlorine was working wonders on their once white feathers. I was about to take a stand when the pool lady took it for me.

Part of The Good Life of California is based on the fer-

vent conviction that if someone else can do it, let him. That's
what leisure is all about. Colonel Sanders, McDonald's, Taco
Pete's, Chili Chuck's, *ad nauseam,* free the housewife from
the strains of a self-cleaning oven. Sixty thousand paid gardeners handle Los Angeles' crab grass and driveway-clean-
ing chores, while encounter groups, swap parties, and hard-
core pornography free either mate of marital obligations. In
a like fashion, for the county's sixty-eight thousand pool owners there is "we'll do it for you" service.

Thrice a week, at about three dollars a visit, a young man
drops by with chlorine, vacuum cleaner, a skimming net, and
soap and brush for the tiles. When he leaves, the pool is
cleaner than most bathtubs. In fact, they do such a sparkling
job, the day is probably not far off when one enterprising
pool service will offer to take care of another local status
symbol, the huge Grecian tubs in His and Her bathrooms.

Ten years before braless picket lines, five-foot-one, two-
hundred-pound June broke the all-male ranks of pool custo-
dians to become the first of her kind in California. June was
an Iowa schoolteacher who had come West to get away from
the corn and "once I finally got here, I sure as hell wasn't going to spend all these beautiful days cooped up with a
bunch of dumb bastards who didn't know their ABCs. I fig-
ured why the hell should guys have all the easy jobs?" As
she circled the pool in short shorts, other bits of personal history, advice, and Hollywood gossip—we learned of immi-
nent divorces when Joyce Haber was still reporting on the
couple's wedding—poured out of June as freely as the smoke
and ashes from the constant cigarette glued to her lower
lip.

The ash-coated water was easy to forget, for June loved
our animals. And they took real love. Brinks was forever
spilling bottles of chemicals in her truck, or swimming about
the pool fouling skimming nets and hose lines. As for the
three Danes, they couldn't wait for cleaning days to play
"Let's push June in the pool." While one barked encourage-
ment, the other two butted hot pants with foreheads. They

never quite succeeded, but several times I caught her playing safe by working from a sitting position along the edge of the water. However, when it came to the ducks, she wasn't taking it sitting down. "Sorry, Eszter"—west of the Rockies, formality breeds contempt—"you either get rid of those damn ducks or look for another pool man. If you want, they can shack up with my chickens until you get straightened out around here and fence in a spot for 'em."

We accepted, but the snail problem remained. June solved that too. "Didn't you know beer is the only way to get rid of snails? They love the stuff so much they get dead drunk, and I mean dead."

While Eszter listened to further details about this very humane method of snail control, I drove down to the market for a couple of six-packs. There is a passable brew in California labeled Colt .45. Considering what we had in mind, it seemed the right brand to buy.

That evening we set out the alcoholic bait. Snails being rather slow pub crawlers, we nestled about a dozen pie tins among the ivy shoots and filled them to the brim with Colt .45. Each neighborhood had its own local bar.

The morning after, we walked down to Gin Row, expecting to see a grisly tableau depicting the wages of Demon Drink. The snails had gotten drunk, all right. The cardiograph of their tracks on the driveway settled that point. But dead, *dead* drunk? No. Genocide of lemming proportions? Hardly. A dozen or so of the underage snails had quaffed too much, fallen in their drink, and drowned. A few of the older, heavier fellows had gone down the same way, but countless others were now safely home sleeping it off under some dark, damp leaf. Since it takes more than one night's indiscretion to make an alcoholic, we would have continued the experiment had not the Danes come home that evening with foam on their muzzles and mirth in their eyes.

4

One Basket

With the same regularity that the workmen showed in coming around for their weekly paycheck, came letters from my mother cautioning against putting all *my* money into Eszter's *hobby:* the house. In a rare display of wit, she finally sent an admonishing telegram addressed to: "One Basket, Coldwater Canyon."

What the worried widow did not know was that the basket was empty. All the eggs were broke and so were we. It was then that Eszter first quoted a Hungarian saying which has since become the family motto: "Wish we could afford to live the way we do." Just before that lament became a dirge, Eszter was commissioned to redesign a house in Beverly Hills (the woman asked Eszter if she was an "inside decorator") and I started a five-year hitch as Executive Program Director of M-G-M Television. The workmen threw a small cocktail party in the garage to celebrate our full employment.

By the time I arrived at Metro you respected and took pride in the studio for what it had been, not for what it was. The proxy fights were already under way for the bounty that was to be made by selling the land, the mother lode of pictures to television, the costumes, the props, and the riverboat that had been Metro-Goldwyn-Mayer. A liquor baron, a real estate king, and the owner of an airline were on safari to bag the roaring lion. Hollywood's most exciting, creative dream factory was living on borrowed time, paying day-to-day expenses by remaking *Dr. Kildare, Father of the Bride,* and *Please Don't Eat the Daisies* into television series. Along with the smog, a blanket of nervous doom shrouded the studio. For me at least, this miasma was swept away each evening as Eszter drove up to the Irving Thalberg Building for the ride home. She had the top down. Dorka and Iago sat in the back seat, necks craning, like every other tourist on a guided tour of "a famous Hollywood film studio." In case my secretary or I missed their grand entrance, the policeman at the gate, Dan Hollywood, on my word, would phone in, "They've arrived."

Dorka loved these nightly excursions and I don't think it was simply a question of getting out of the house. She behaved like any other would-be actress looking for a part. Every man—i.e., a possible producer or casting director— who walked past the car was given either a come-hither look or a good shot of her profile. Dorka was not vamping this way solely on her own. She got encouraging smiles and cuing nudges from Eszter. "Well, didn't Lassie and that sheep dog in *Daisies* get their big break at Metro? Why couldn't Dorka make it?" She was beginning to sound like every other stage mother in town. Before the two of them went off to buy a rhinestone collar or a pair of tap-dancing shoes, I explained that medical, not veterinarian, shows were then the vogue. And besides, M-G-M had a firm rule against nepotism.

Iago put on none of these stage-struck airs, probably for the same reason an actor with a recent face lift steers clear of the studios until the scars have healed. The dog's ears were still up in those white conical bandages which make a young Dane look like a unicorn carrying a spare.

Rousseau was not a member of those studio tours for the

same reason we were still a one-car family—economics. Iago's look-alike brother—if you are not the sort that snoops between toes to uncover a few flecks of white—was sent back East to a fan of Dorka's who had once said, "If Dorka is ever bred, promise I get one of the litter, even if it's the runt." It would have been fun to see her expression when a 99%10 per cent black harlequin came bouncing out of the crate.

That casting one six-month-old puppy from house and home should make a difference in the budget is hard to believe, but here is the annual cupboard inventory for one medium-size Great Dane in his first year. Read and whimper.

The Larder:	*Per Annum*
Horsemeat—15 lbs. a week @ 42¢ per pound	$327.60
Cottage cheese—3 qts. a week @ 68¢ per qt.	106.08
Hard-boiled eggs—1 doz. a week @ 39¢ per doz.	20.28
Liver (ends)—2 lbs. a week @ 49¢ per lb.	50.96
Kibble—50 lbs. a month @ $4.95 per bag	59.40
"Milkbones" (5 at bedtime)—49¢ per box	25.48
Bone bones—1 a day, 15¢ for a bag of four	13.65
Soy oil—1 tbsp. a day, 1 bottle a month @ 69¢	8.28
Salt & garlic salt (to taste)	2.00
	$613.73

The Medicine Chest:	
Pervinal (vitamins)—9 lbs. a year	$ 25.00
Calcium—15 lbs. a year	13.50
Flea powder (for bedding)	2.75
Flea collars (California's tick season outlasts the guarantee.)—2 @ $1.95	3.90
Distemper shots—2 @ $8.50	17.00
Hepatitis shot	6.00
Ear cropping	40.00
Office visit to Dr. Sprowl ("Why isn't the Dane eating?" "He's teething.")	5.00
" " " " " ("Why is the dog constantly hungry?" "He stopped teething.")	5.00
" " " " " (Dane swallowed license tags.)	5.00
	$123.15

Miscellaneous:

Two sets of L.A. license tags	$ 7.00
Two collars for growing necks	5.00
One leather leash	4.50
One chain lead to replace above (masticated)	5.00
Rubber balls for chewing up, burying, or losing	3.00
One guest's leather handbag (destroyed) *	45.00
	$ 69.50
GRAND TOTAL:	$806.38

About three days after Rousseau had taken the night flight to New York, Eszter was late picking me up at work. No dogs in the car, and not only was the top up, all the windows were closed. Very strange for a balmy California evening. As I walked closer to the car, it became evident why the convertible was sealed. On every square inch of floor and seat were flats of tender spring plants.

Peeved at having had to wait, I grumbled, "You're late."

"Get in quickly."

"That's not going to make you less late."

Eszter was hugging her chest. There seemed to be more than the usual bulge in that area. "Please hurry, you're leaving the door open." I got in, transferring a flat of petunias to my lap and wedging my feet between some potted geraniums. My shoes made a crunchy sound.

"That's just kitty litter. The bag broke."

"But we don't have cats."

"Yes, we do." And on perfect cue Eszter's bosoms began to meow. A second later, out of the décolletage crept two Siamese kittens. They were both rather mangy and terribly thin. The boy was called Pancake, the girl we named Petunia. Never particularly fond of cats, I really did not want to hold the kittens, but neither was I anxious for them to crawl back into Eszter's dress when she was driving. We compromised. I held them at near arm's length—like sacrifices to the gods—while Eszter acted out the heart-rending scene

---

* Average vandalism for a well-trained dog. However, for a master of conspicuous consumption see GBS's eating habits, Chapter 15.

of finding Pancake and Petunia abandoned in the nursery-man's potting shed.

"I had to take them both. How would you feel if you were separated from your family?" Knowing how Eszter felt about my mother, it was a poor choice of questions.

"Why didn't his wife take them in?"

"She's allergic."

"You know, I think I am, too." Had my hands not been full of poison, I would have rubbed my eyes. They were starting to tear and itch.

"Don't be silly—it's all mental."

"You're right. I don't like cats."

My aversion was to turn to love, although the itching has never gone away. Over the years, as our coterie of cats grew in size and denominations, Eszter tried everything to stop the allergy, from looking up Christian Science practitioners in the Yellow Pages to buying Neo-Medrol at twelve dollars a tube. The latter works, by the way, no matter what the former may say.

Dorka had that very special faculty—auditory, I am sure —which enabled her to know when our car was navigating the Canyon more than a quarter of a mile away. That evening she and Iago met us at the gate and, like two outriders, raced up the hill to the garage. It was a most demonstrative welcome with a good deal of car thumping and paint scratching. Pancake and Petunia jumped from my hands to the flowers to the shelter of Eszter's arms. Before opening the car door I asked, "Do you think they'll get along?"

Eszter, rather shocked: "Of course. Dorka is a Mother and a Lady."

That was meant to end the inquiry, but since Dorka was now demantling the windshield wiper in a most unladylike fashion while Iago had the antenna bent to an inverted U, I couldn't resist asking, "Where did that expression 'fighting like cats and dogs' come from?"

"That's just about men and women."

While I unloaded the flats, Eszter sat on the garage floor

shielding the kittens from the investigating muzzles of the
Danes. What she said to the dogs is far too embarrassing to
repeat verbatim, but they heard a playback of her finding
the cats alone and abandoned and they had to sit through a
special sermon on the obligations of the well-fed and well-
housed to the orphans of the world. When it was over,
Dorka seemed converted and trotted off to the doghouse
for further meditation. Iago followed because he always followed his mother and because he wanted to lick his
wounds, physical and emotional. He had spent the entire
lecture probing the kittens to determine their sex. They found
his bedside manner far too aggressive and undignified and
scratched his black nose until tiny beads of blood appeared.
That such small things could play so rough must have hurt
more than the clawing.

Pancake and Petunia had one further initiation to go
through before becoming full-fledged members of the household—Brinks. Eszter admitted being worried about that
meeting. We went inside to feed the adopted pair.

The workmen had packed up their tools and reluctantly
stolen away about a week before. We were at last in sole possession of such basics as a bedroom, bath, and kitchen. It
was glorious, although after eight months of coexistence with
carpenters and painters the house was now and then haunted
by voices shouting, "Could you come here a minute?" "Do
you have a dustpan and brush?," or, "Is that the color you
wanted? It'll dry different of course."

In deference to my incipient allergy, Eszter agreed that the
kittens were to be bedded down in the kitchen. With a
scratch here and a scratch there, I managed to extend my
victory to a Hungarian pledge that as far as Pancake and Petunia were concerned the rest of the house was off limits.
Phobias aside, it was actually an ideal spot for them. Iago had
outgrown the flapping door which had been installed in the
lower half of the Dutch door that separated kitchen from
garden. As soon as Pancake and Petunia were big enough to
push they could come and go as they pleased.

It was through this swinging door that Brinks appeared that first evening, playing to the teeth the part of Gary Cooper, the wandering stranger, entering the hostile town saloon. His arrival was equally unexpected, since the raccoon's recent nights had been spent trash can hopping around the neighborhood. When he did scurry home about dawn he headed straight for the doghouse to cuddle up between his warm friends, forgoing the luxury of the special bed I had put up for him, a carpet-lined nail keg nestled in the fork of a dead sapling.

With the door still flapping behind him, Brinks gave the kitchen a thorough once-over. On spying the kittens, he did not blink an eye, but his nose winked like mad, giving us all an on-and-off view of his front teeth. I had felt those incisors before and the thought that I might have to unclamp them from Pancake or Petunia made me very apprehensive. Eszter confessed she was frightened, too—for the kittens—but, "they've got to meet sometime."

The two newcomers must have reached the same conclusion, for they came out from behind their plate of chopped liver and walked very cautiously toward the bandit-faced character with the beady-eye stare. With Petunia slightly in the lead, they took their stand about a foot from the raccoon. A three-way long-distance sniffing contest then ensued. Finally Brinks made his move. From all fours he rose to his hind legs, waddled toward Petunia and picked her up in a bear hug. But it was a warm, loving embrace and to show that he meant no harm Brinks commenced doing somersaults and roll-overs with the kitten clasped to his body. Petunia was ecstatic and her brother stood in line purring to be next. This touching performance, a cross between a wrestling match and gymnastics, went on for about ten minutes. Then Brinks exited through the swinging door as quickly as he had entered.

Strangely, this was their first and last physical encounter. From that evening forth the raccoon and the kittens met daily, but our efforts to have Brinks replay the role of foster father were futile. Having showed the loving side of his nature, he was conscience-free to play more devilish games. Like harassing my mother.

Now that the house was finished we were faced with an inescapable fact of life: My mother should be invited. If for no other reason than that she could see where the money was buried. Of course, there were grounds for further procrastination. Remodeling is fittingly akin to falling in love. Once started you are never really finished, nor do you want to be, no matter what you say to the contrary. But Eszter and I could not hide behind that technicality forever. The elephants had vacated the guest room. There were no more excuses. I slipped the invitation into the mailbox with the same speed and trepidation used in testing a tub of hot water.

Eszter and my mother were livid proof that opposites don't necessarily attract. One said what she meant, the other meant what she didn't say. One loved life, the other was afraid of its sensuality. Far more important to the coming visit though was our guest's attitude toward animals.

Mother claimed she liked dogs—cats she wouldn't even talk about—and I am sure she did if they kept their proper place, away from her and preferably up on the movie screen or in novels where dogs went for country walks with their pipe-smoking masters or protected helpless widows from black rapists. If she had to come in actual contact with the creatures, it was mandatory that they be on a leash, wipe their feet before entering, shower daily, have a shed-proof coat, and never salivate. Above all, dogs should be small. Had God wanted them big, He would have made them horses.

Dorka and Iago accompanied Eszter to the airport to pick up our visitor. To my regret and Eszter's fury, I remembered a very unimportant meeting which would keep me from going along. That evening I asked about the happy reunion. (For the duration of Mother's visit almost all private conversations took place in our bathroom behind a closed

door. Rather paranoic behavior on our part, since our guest
was very hard of hearing.)

"How'd it go?"

"How did what go?"

"Your meeting."

"Fine." Eszter never uses that word unless something has
happened.

"What about the dogs?"

"*They* like her very much."

"Where is she now?"

"Cleaning her jacket. Iago kept trying to kiss her and I guess
a little drool dripped."

Not wanting to hear any more, I started to leave. Eszter
stopped me: "You don't have to feed the dogs tonight."
Pause. "Beth [it was *your* mother when she was angry]
brought us a house present of six New York-cut steaks.
While I was carrying her luggage in, they found the box."

"When courting, or fleeing an argument, always dine out.
A good restaurant is private enough to foster the first and
public enough to quash the second." The aphorism is from
the lips of a friend thrice divorced; nevertheless, on this in-
augural evening going out for dinner seemed the wisest move.
We went to Scandia, the finest restaurant west of New York
and one of the few places in town where patrons may
choose the room with the candlepower by which they wish
to dine.

Eating in almost total darkness is the only distinctive quality about Los Angeles restaurants. Even at high noon, the cap-
tain must lead you by the hand to your table. Several enterprising restaurateurs have cut down on the cost of flashlight
batteries by adding and totaling your check with a nite-glo
pen. There are divergent theories to explain the cavelike
mentality behind these blackouts. Some say that after a day
in the sun and blinding smog it is the best way to rest your
eyes. Others, that it is a hangover from the "old Hollywood"
when it was pretty daring for a film star to be seen with a

woman other than his wife. Now, of course, the only way to make the gossip columns is to be caught with her. There is a last, more ingenious, reason given for the low voltage: Should a gentleman be dining with the wrong woman when the right woman enters the establishment, in the long minute it takes for the latter to adjust her eyes from sunlight to no light the guilty party can hurry out through the kitchen or play a waiting game in the men's room.

I give some credence to this view, having noticed that the most suspect of swingers are usually seated facing the front door. However, the right explanation is more mundane than any of these. Quite simply and sadly, the chefs are so bad in Los Angeles that they have insisted upon the inclusion of a clause in their labor contracts which states that the dining room lighting must be low enough to prevent customers from comparing what is served with what was ordered.

Getting back to our properly illuminated dinner. It was a great success. Mother was effusive in her praise of the poached turbot and our house. We did not mention the animals and she never brought up the missing house present or expounded on her anti-one-basket philosophy. By the time we had gotten home and delivered her to the door of the guest room, I was starting to believe that the next few weeks might go well after all. Or, at least, not badly.

Eszter and I were halfway through the house on the way to our bedroom, when my dreams of a cease-fire were shattered by a terrifying series of screams. They were so hysterical and high-pitched that the dogs started howling an accompaniment, as they do when a fire engine or ambulance is heard in the Canyon. We ran back to the guest room.

From the top of the steps we saw Mother splayed out against one wall, wide, wild eyes fixed upon the center of her bed. There sat Brinks, taking an inventory of her handbag. He had everything turned out on the bed, including a package of Metrecal cookies Mother had been secretly carrying as possible protection against Eszter's cooking. Brinks downed these wafers one by one, stopping between bites to play with such exciting new toys as hearing aid batteries, traveler's checks, a package of Mylanta tablets, and a bottle of Binaca. He started on the last as soon as the cookies were finished.

Eszter contained herself long enough to assure Beth, "It's only a raccoon. Don't worry, he's our friend and *lives with us.*" She then raced into the guest bath, turned on the faucets, and burst into laughter. When she came out, there were tears in her eyes. The wrong sort. The scene was that funny, though, and I had difficulty suppressing my smiles as I reassured Mother that living with us meant "living out-doors" and that the raccoon must have slipped through her open window. It would not happen again. When Eszter picked Brinks up to put him outside, she whispered, "Don't be afraid, poor Brinksie." My mother read lips perfectly.

There was not to be peace in our time.

Food, or more precisely the quantity of it, was another bone of contention between Eszter and Beth. The latter was a staunch believer that the way to a man's heart was through his stomach. Eszter thought this Victorian theory was merely a form of sexual sublimation and, more important, that it was the quickest route to a man's heart attack. My stomach be-came the battlefield upon which their war of calories was to be fought.

California has made me an early riser by choice—and neces-sity. There are so many lovely things to see and do before the confinement of the office. While the water boils for coffee, the dogs and I walk down to the gate for the paper. Along the way they chase squirrels, birds, their tails—anything that moves. This is the time I love best. Our world is so quiet and freshly new. The sun is starting to burn through the morning fog and everywhere I look are Eszter's plantings celebrating another day of life. The Iceland poppies struggling out of their pods, the millions of tiny yellow flowers weighing down the acacia trees, and the orchard, full of orange and peach trees just starting to bloom. All this on a morning in mid-January. No Easterner ever gets quite used to that.

While the Danes race back up the driveway carrying the newspaper—Dorka is in charge of the parts we want to read, leaving Iago free to chew over the sports and financial sections—I stop to pick oranges for breakfast and a lemon for cocktail time. But there is a price for these daily sessions of garden watching, for I also notice a weekendful of chores which must be done. The citrus and avocado should be cultivated, the border of white oleanders along the drive needs shaping, and some damn deliveryman has backed over a section of sprinkler pipe.

When I returned to the kitchen the morning after The Great Metrecal Robbery, there was Mother going through all the cabinets and drawers.

"Can I help you find something?"

"No. Eszter said she was going shopping today. I thought I'd make a list of what you need." Looking at the pad in her hand, I saw she was starting on her third page.

"I don't see any baking pans or a flour sifter."

This was as good a time as any to explain that I was watching my weight and Eszter was helping me. Dinners consisted of a huge salad and vegetables along with broiled meat or chicken and very few desserts. Omitting the last was a most noble sacrifice on Eszter's part, since she loves nothing more than rich chocolate pastry, or chestnut purée, covered with a foot of whipped cream.

Having been deaf myself, I knew from practice that there is nothing easier for the hard of hearing than to tune out a conversation. Mother's reply to my diet speech was a case in point.

"Is that all you're going to have for breakfast, orange juice and coffee?"

"That's all I want."

"You know, dear, I didn't want to say anything in front of your wife, but you do look terribly thin. Why, I remember when you used to have pancakes and hot cereal every morning."

"That was when I was twelve years old, my schoolmates called me 'Chubby,' and I spent one Saturday a month in the doctor's office having my thyroid checked." She started on page four of the shopping list.

During that evening's conference in the bathroom, I felt it prudent to turn on the faucets, the shower, *and* flush the toilet.

"Don't bother paying the mortgage this month; we'll never live to see the first of February. Do you know what we did today?"

"Went shopping."

"Foraging for an army, you mean. Would you believe that that woman, your mother, spent one hundred and eighty dollars and eighty-seven cents on food and baking utensils? I have the Blue Chip stamps to prove it. I'm warning you: When you open the refrigerator, stand back or you'll be caught in an avalanche."

"Where's your sense of humor?"

"In the deep freeze along with three cheesecakes, three gallons of ice cream, and three six-rib roasts. I could maybe understand if she was a compulsive eater or fat beyond recall; but no, there she stands not an ounce overweight, debating whether to buy her son *croissants* or apple Danish and settling for both. And then when we get home she won't have anything but cottage cheese and yogurt for lunch."

"Why didn't you say no?"

"I did and that's when she started buying three of everything."

"Don't turn off the faucets, I want to wash up. It must be time for dinner?"

"I wouldn't know. Madame Bountiful asked if she could fix you a 'home-cooked' meal. She made it sound as though Colonel Sanders was our resident chef."

"I'm sorry. Come on, let's face it." And hand in hand we wandered down Cholesterol Alley.

As bread dough rose on the counter and cakes climbed high in the oven, so did the tension. Our nerves were becoming as mushy as Mother's whipped potatoes, our hearts as heavy. Eszter soon realized that there was no getting through to a hearing aid permanently set at "off." She capitulated. "The siege of Budapest was nothing compared to this. How long do you think we'll be occupied?"

It looked like a long haul, for in that morning's mail the New York *Times* and the *Wall Street Journal* arrived. Mother had changed her mailing address.

The days that followed were best forgotten and Eszter tried to do just that by sleeping later and later each morning. When the two adversaries met in the middle of the kitchen, there were overly polite good mornings and then Eszter took her breakfast out to the doghouse, where Dorka and Iago had been spending more and more of their time, by choice, aware of the conflict in our house. After her coffee and dog talk, Eszter would go off to her studio for the day or work until dark on the gardens which were to surround the house, concentric waves of pure primary colors that splashed against the brick terrace and white stucco walls.

Except for the days when Eszter served as chauffeur on silent shopping expeditions, the car was mine. Coming home each night, I no longer had to get out and open the garage door. It was done by Mother, who stood watching, from six o'clock on, for the car lights at the gate. This evening vigil guaranteed that she would be first with her version of the day's battle of attrition. In the bathroom, moments later, I would hear the home team's report. God, in His benevolence, has allowed me to block out all but two of these charge and countercharge scenes.

The first took place in the garage. Time: the moment I shut off the ignition. Principal Character: Mother, paler than usual.

"Good evening, dear. Your wife has bugs."

"Now, come on. Enough is enough. Please let me out of the car."

She took two steps back from the door. "I'm serious. The place is full of them."

"What place?"

"Shush. Follow me. Be very quiet." Either they were still alive or, more likely, she did not want Eszter to hear of this latest victory—just yet. I followed her toward the second-hand refrigerator we keep in a corner of the garage, reserved for pet food. As she pulled open the door, I remembered.

A friend had given us a wonderful Christmas present— five thousand frozen ladybugs. In a month or so, when spring arrived and the aphids started attacking the citrus, we were to thaw out the bugs from their big sleep and sprinkle them about the orchard. The lady in Oregon who commercially raises the insects must have a very motherly heart, for on each pastry-size box of one thousand there is a cautionary label: Be sure to water the foliage first before broadcasting the bugs. It seems that after their period of hibernation the ladies can't wait for a pick-me-up.

When Mother swung shut the freezer section with a bang of victory, I explained, "They're ladybugs. We are going to use them instead of DDT."

"Why are you always making up stories to protect that woman?"

My second memory of those evening news reports seems to follow the equal-time doctrine; it is a story of Eszter's that I recall. On this occasion my evening briefing session was not orchestrated to the sound of running water. The situation had reached such an impasse that our concern was now focused on the escalating water bill. Eszter said, "You get the drinks. I'll meet you in the doghouse."

Out of guilt and compassion, I had gotten in the habit of bringing home some little present. That night it was a single white rose.

"Thank you, darling. It will look lovely on my grave. Promise, though, that you won't invite her to the funeral?"

With the dogs staring up at me, I was more aware than ever of how silent I had become during these meetings.

"I spent all day on the blue garden in the front of the house. After lunch, Beth came out with a broom and asked me to move the dogs, who were sitting on the drive keeping me company. Simple Hungarian peasant that I am, I asked if they were bothering her. No, but she was going to sweep the drive. Idiot that I am, I asked why and got an answer, 'Somebody has to keep this place tidy.'" (The drive is over a thousand feet long and fifteen feet wide.) "No wait, the best is yet to come. About six, when she came out again to wait for you-know-who's headlights, I had just put in the last plant. She looked over the new garden with great satisfaction and said, so help me God, 'Well, you've earned your keep—today.' In another week I'll be saying 'Yas'm' and curtsying." I would have laughed, but Eszter was obviously close to tears.

"Bruce, please, you've got to do something."

"What? I can't very well say, 'Mother, go home.'"

In his own inimitable way, Brinks said it for me.

Instead of going straight home to Iago and Dorka one morning the raccoon made a predawn detour down our chimney. He had done it once before and I usually kept the damper closed, but in January the evenings often get down to thirty degrees—fireplace weather. Brinks's soot marks led straight to the guest's bath, where it was clear that he had washed up with a mixture of Mother's various night creams and Swiss Kress. His greasy, ashen tracks then led to the guest room, across the floor, and up onto the bed. When Mother awoke she sensed that there was something behind her head other than a pillow. Brinks had fallen asleep in the warmth of her hair. Too proud to call for help this time, Beth tried swatting him away. It took several minutes before Brinks untangled his paws from her hair net and scurried off, back up the chimney.

I heard the details of the night's visitation on the way to the airport. For, by the time I arrived in the kitchen at six-thirty, Mother's bags were packed and at the front door. Dressed for her journey East in a chic Norell suit and a fur hat, she was standing at the stove making me a stack of wheat cakes. I ate them.

That night we got on the scale. In little less than four weeks, I had gained fourteen pounds. Eszter had lost almost ten and Mother would have weighed out even. As the animals had suffered by our guest's presence, so were they recompensed by her absence. Instead of kibble, Iago and Dorka feasted on cake and bread mixed with their horsemeat. And as a special treat they were given the bags of turkey stuffing Mother had prepared and laid away in the freezer. Pancake and Petunia inherited a huge enamel roasting pan to hold kitty litter, and the cookie sheets made ideal trays for their water and feed bowls. Eszter rewarded Brinks by using up the gallon of maple syrup on his daily meal of chicken wings and fish scraps. As for the flour sifter? It is still being used for dusting the rose bushes.

I only saw Mother once again. From time to time letters were exchanged, the ones people write who are afraid to ask questions. Then, three years later, I went to Paris to try to salvage what should have been a wonderful television series, "Harry's Girls." At the same time, I learned that Mother was lying in a Zurich hospital, dying of cancer. I went to visit her.

Mother had never consciously hurt anyone. She should not have been made to suffer so. She was in too much pain to talk very much and I was at a loss for things to say. Certainly Beth did not want to hear about the problems of a television comedy series that was completely devoid of laughs, or what Eszter was doing back in California. She helped me out. Raising an arm with great effort, Mother gently patted her hair and smiled. "Tell me all about Brinks."

5

Incest by the Pool

As befits a beautiful grandame, we had remodeled the whole front of the house to accommodate the three-hundred-year-old live California oak. Two eight-by-ten skylights were set into the roof, so that from either the living room or the dining area we could look up at a massive green and silver cloud. Outside, a brick terrace was put down extending beneath the far reaches of its limbs and the trunk, easily fifteen feet in circumference, was encircled with a brick bench. That was the year the old lady showed no inclination to put on her leaf-green spring mantle. We called a tree surgeon.

After a half-dozen spinal taps, a good deal of trunk thumping, and careful analysis of bark samples, he reported his findings. This was no ordinary patient and it was with genuine sorrow that he announced, "I'm afraid she's dead. Has been for some time, I'd say. Last year's leaves were what you might call a final spasm, a desperate try at hanging on. I know how you must feel." Cause of death: smog poisoning. Man had done in two decades what three centuries of drought, fire, and earthquakes could not manage.

We felt lonely and hollow contemplating what the place

would look like without the shady giant. Something had to be done and we were neither stoical nor young enough to wait fifty years for a poor facsimile to grow. Eszter asked the tree man how long we could keep the bare oak tree from falling down. "If you pour cement around the base to hold the roots, cut back the secondary branches, and we don't have any bad windstorms, I'd guess seven years." (For the unbelievable accuracy of that prediction, see Chapter 10.)

Along with 100 million other Americans, Eszter considers seven her private lucky number. This conviction, however, has nothing to do with the fact that she was born a Libra, the seventh sign of the zodiac. For as far as she is concerned, astrology is as accurate as a gypsy fortuneteller and nowhere near as amusing. "How can there be anything to it, when Libra is the only sign not connected with an animal?" But the tree surgeon had said seven, so Eszter had the roots buried in a truckload of concrete, cut off the more precarious branches, and called the nursery for seven red bougainvillea. I was on the phone next to ask our insurance agent to double the wind damage coverage on the house. If that tree ever fell on the roof . . .

When the bougainvillea arrived, Eszter planted them at the foot of the oak and started training the vines up the trunk. Her regimen of force-feeding with hormones and liquid fertilizers was so successful that by the following spring I had to use a twenty-foot ladder to tie the vines to the dead limbs. *Voilà,* a red and green parasol popped open over the house.

Aesthetics was not sole reason for trying to resurrect the California oak; it had become Brinks's jungle gym and hideout. After perpetrating some particularly heinous crime, he would make his getaway along the upper limbs and hole up behind a curtain of leaves. I discovered this route and the impossibility of getting to him the morning I found his paw prints all over the car windshield—and the keys missing. It happened to be on a day when I had an early meeting with the head of the studio. I was an hour late. Robert Weitman was not glad to see me. "What happened, did the Danes borrow the car?"

"No, the raccoon stole the keys." He just looked at me. "Really, Bob, and then he climbed to the top of that old oak tree of ours and he wouldn't give them back." He stared at me a little longer, and then: "Why don't you just leave quietly? We can have our meeting another time." I backed out.

The shadow Brinks had cast upon my veracity was lifted a month or so later.

I decided that the only way to dispel that oh-it's-you look I was getting around the Thalberg Building and commissary was to have the Weitmans for dinner and during cocktails we could have Brinks in to say goodnight to the guests, just in case Bob doubted the animal's existence. It was all right to be taken for an animal lover, but an imaginary animal lover was another thing. The Weitmans came and I prepared the drinks, but no raccoon. This was very unusual, for every day at drink time the fellow would appear out of nowhere to have his own special *apéritif*—one raw egg. Sitting on his haunches, he cradled the egg between his paws, very neatly made a hole in the top with his teeth and then, throwing his head back, slurped down the contents in one swallow. Of all nights, Brinks had chosen this one to go on the wagon.

We sat down for dinner. Halfway through the salad, all the lights in that section of the house went out. I headed for the kitchen to check the fuse box. A few seconds later, in answer to my "come quick," the Weitmans and Eszter were standing beside me and heard me triumphantly announce, "See, there really is a Brinks."

The raccoon had gotten to the circuit box, pried open the door latch, and was systematically unscrewing each fuse. Everyone was so fascinated that we stood there while the raccoon went on to darken the kitchen, bringing down the curtain on his own performance. Eszter lit some candles and broke the silence:

"Good show, Brinks, but I've got to fix the chicken. Bruce will put you out."

That was not my favorite duty. I had never gotten over the toothy experience of sleeping with the animal and when bodily contact between the two of us was unavoidable I took certain cowardly precautions which had been kept a family secret. I would have preferred to show Brinks the door without an audience. But no, the Weitmans were having much too good a time and showed no desire to go back to the dinner table. "Hurry up, Bruce. I'm almost ready," Eszter said.

I took my tools of fear from the kitchen cabinet: a pair of heavy asbestos gloves, the gauntlet kind worn by telephone linemen which almost reach to the elbow, and an old army blanket. I slipped on the former and, holding the blanket like a bullfighter's cape, advanced toward my adversary. With four or five safe feet separating us, I cast the blanket over the four pounds of fur. Then, swaddling him in my gloved and blanket-padded hands, I deposited Brinks in the middle of the terrace, being careful to keep both eyes on him while retreating. When I backed into the kitchen that night, Bob Weitman asked, "Who gets the ear, Belmonte?"

We put a lock and key on the fuse box, but for every toy taken away, the raccoon found another. Which brings me back to the oak tree for a moment. When the old lady lost the last of her leaves, Brinks no longer had a curtained hideaway where he could sleep off the excitement of his latest caper. Now he needed some sort of physical therapy to calm him down. He discovered it in the large strips of bark which were beginning to peel from the tree. With a little clawing he found he could strip off large chunks of the heavy, woody stuff. Then came the real fun—dropping them on the heads of cats, dogs, and guests below. Brinks became such an accurate bombardier that during outdoor lunches on the terrace we put an umbrella under the bougainvillea umbrella.

Iago was becoming a magnificent animal, broad-chested and sleek-coated. Not yet a year old, his head already matched Dorka's in size and breadth. Both ears stood at at-

tention, curving slightly inward so that the tips touched to
form a black arch over his soft brown eyes. Once a month I
would pick him up and step on the bathroom scale, while
Eszter squatted under my armful to read the dial. The lifting
part was becoming more and more of a strain and we had to
call it quits when Eszter proclaimed, "You weigh three hundred pounds." A hundred and thirty-five of that belonged to
Iago.

Our pride in Iago's development exposed us to one of man's
least harmful but silliest vanities—the dog show. It was not
surprising, what with all the touring about they did in the
back of the convertible, that Dorka and Iago should come to
the attention of other Dane lovers. They all urged that the
dogs be entered in the upcoming Long Beach Dog Show in
Orange County, one of the largest in the country. Two suede-
skirted, cardigan-topped ladies from the local chapter of the
Great Dane Club of America came up to the house to coach
Eszter and the dogs on how best to show off. Dorka and
Eszter were quick studies, but Iago seemed to feel that all this
standing about with your legs spread out was both tiring and
embarrassing. He sat down a lot. The ladies told us not to
worry, because it was Dorka they were really interested in.
Harlequins were still a rarity on the West Coast, while black
Danes were considered by the judges to be less desirable than
fawns or brindles. That was a year or so before the slogan
"Black Is Beautiful," but it was obvious from the angry look
in her eyes that Eszter planned to get that message across, to
integrate Orange County thinking.

The show was on a Sunday. Saturday night I had four baths.
One with, and one after, each of the dogs. Then Eszter took
over, drying them in front of the fireplace. This was followed
by one of those acts which, if committed by a man, is called
cheating; if by a woman, it is sloughed off as feminine wile.
To be sure that the judges would see only Dorka's spots before their eyes, Eszter dusted her coat with white talcum
powder and then shined up each black area with Johnson's
Baby Oil. The art work had to be repeated in the morning; for

during the night while they slept side by side, Dorka had transferred her spots to Iago. Now that there was no possibility that the judges would overlook Dorka, it was imperative that they have no trouble finding Eszter when the moment came to award the blue ribbons. She had provided: she had knitted a special black-and-white-spotted sweater for the occasion.

Dorka took first place in both of her classes. She and Eszter received a standing ovation. Most of the audience had never seen a harlequin before nor, for that matter, a class in which only one dog was entered. Any loneliness Dorka may have felt parading around the ring by herself soon vanished. The moment the class was over, she was petted by a long line of Dane owners asking her hand in marriage on behalf of their studs. To each, Eszter replied that Dorka was spoken for. I didn't have time to ask by whom, or why, because Iago's class was next.

Iago of Dorkadane, as he was officially registered, had slightly stiffer competition than his mother. Thirty-four other puppies were competing, mostly brindles and fawns. With Iago, the black minority numbered three. Eszter stripped down to fighting weight for this color contest. Taking off her spotted sweater, she entered the ring in a miniskirted dress of black-and-white ticking. As she and Iago walked around and around and around, Iago's ears started a slow descent. Eszter flashed her look of wiles and I began walking around and around, hiding behind one and then another spectator, making slightly illegal clucking sounds to keep Iago's ears aloft. He heard me, but the judges were too busy brushing fuzz off their blazers to notice the deceit. Iago placed second. Eszter's slight disappointment vanished in a laugh when I told her that the American Kennel Club will not allow white German shepherds even to enter the show ring.

Driving home, we decided that it had been fun but once was enough. The dog show circuit was for people who liked Sunday traffic and wanted to get away from home on weekends. Which reminded me:

"Speaking of things I don't want to do again, what was that remark, back at the show, about breeding Dorka?"

"I'd like to have one of Iago's sons someday, wouldn't you?"

"Yes, but that's Iago. You were talking about Dorka."

"Where could we find a more beautiful mate for him? And they really do love each other."

"I thought inbreeding went out with the Borgias."

"They say you can do it once without spoiling the blood-line."

"Who's you in this case?"

"You. I'll show you how we did it in Downey."

It turned out that the real question was who was going to show Iago.

Two months later Dorka was in heat. For the past week she had been locked up in the guest room, safe from Iago's pre-nuptial advances. I don't know why I decided that the pool deck should be the site for the ceremony, but it proved a wise choice. Eszter took Dorka down to the pool and made a bed for her by spreading some towels over a beach pad. Up at the house, I was holding Iago firmly by his leash. For seven days and nights he had spent his time yowling a lovesick re-frain outside the guest room window.

Eszter called out, "Okay, we're ready."

Hearing her voice, Iago broke loose and raced toward the girls.

"Look out, he's coming."

Instead of being witness to a scene of lascivious abandon, when I arrived at the pool area a minute later, there were the two Danes exchanging quite innocent, platonic kisses. With these hellos over, Iago walked down the steps into the pool and swam a few lengths.

"What's he doing that for?"

"He's a gentleman. Taking a shower before making love."

Eszter was wrong. Iago was swimming, period. After a few more laps he got out, lay down by himself in the sun, and went to sleep. I was both relieved and disappointed.

"Now what?"

"How do I know? Maybe he's resting."

"Before?" As though in answer to the insult, Iago got up and walked over to Dorka, where some very serious sniffing took place. Eszter had been privy to these warning signs before:

"Get ready. I'll hold Dorka's head. You help Iago find the right position."

I wish that the four Harvard professors who had given me my oral examination in philosophy had been present to observe this field lesson in pragmatism. One student, Class of '47, had taken a crooked turn. I lifted and nudged and pushed and said, "That's right, Iago," and, "No, Iago," and, "Wait, Iago," but we couldn't make the coupling. Both of us were feeling a little frightened and very faint.

Eszter, standing up front, opened her eyes long enough to ask, "What's wrong?"

"His back legs seem to be too short."

"Try propping them up."

On the deck was one of those Styrofoam floats in the shape of a cake of Ivory soap. I placed it under his rear legs. It was just the right elevation, but poor nervous Iago had a premature ejaculation. The towel, not Dorka, became impregnated with semen. In a last desperate and futile try at poolside gynecology, I wiped Dorka's vagina with the wet towel. Eszter opened her eyes and quickly shut them:

"I think he wants to try some more."

He did, but I surely didn't, not ever again. I dragged Iago away and into the pool, where we both sat at the children's end cooling off. Eszter had no trouble getting sweet, patient Dorka to follow her back to the guest room.

When her period of forced celibacy was over, Dorka moved out and Gordon Parks moved in to photograph the "House of Flowers" story for *Life* magazine. The idea had been Shana Alexander's, a brilliant writer and friend beyond the calls of friendship, a woman who loved flowers and embroidery. Eszter had nurtured fields of both.

Gordon had a thing about large dogs and when Dorka and

Iago stormed out to greet him for the first time, it found a name: "Fear." Eszter hurried to chaperon him to the house: "Don't worry, Gordon. You can bet a million dollars that they'd never hurt you."

To seal the wager, Dorka nosed her way through dangling tripods and swinging camera cases to clasp him on the calf. Iago stood by, learning how it was done.

"She's just playing, honest. Don't worry."

Gordon did worry, and limp, for the next three days. He voluntarily placed himself under house arrest. Unable to rest outside, Dorka's territory, between photographs, he set up typewriter and Remy Martin bottle in the guest room and worked away at his first novel, *The Burning Tree*. Gordon, the book, and the pictures of our life were beautiful. As a measure of the man, one of the loveliest photographs in the whole story is of his enemy, Dorka.

Shana was connected far more closely with another occasion when Dorka made her presence felt. Steve, her husband, had just produced his first movie and we were invited to a "sneak" preview (nothing, including released films, is better advertised in Hollywood than these secret screenings). They would pick us up. When the gate bell rang, we were still dressing and by the time I turned on the lights and went outside it was too late. While Paramount's longest and blackest chauffeur-driven limousine was still moving to a stop, Steve had jumped out. He and Dorka were old friends, true; but Dorka had never seen a car of such ominous magnitude before and it, coupled with Steve's Batman entrance in complete darkness, was too much to take. So Dorka got a firm grip on the mysterious intruder's knee and it was several long seconds before she would consent to let go. Steve's trousers were torn and bloodstained. I publicly punished Dorka and she crept away in shame. Privately, I felt sorry for the bewildered animal and it hurt me to have hit her. She had been trying to protect us and her young son from a silent intruder. Had Steve said something before leaping from the car, had she

heard his familiar voice, Dorka would not have attacked. She
never did again.

It was not until after the screening, and the pain was severe,
that Steve would accept medical attention. I do not mean to
imply that the movie acted as an anesthesia until then. Drains
were put in his knee. Dorka was put in quarantine. We had
to keep her behind the gate for ten days, during which time
a health inspector made periodic checks to be sure she was
not rabid. And a large ominous red sign was placed on the
gate warning one and all to beware of a possibly dangerous
animal. Although Dorka received a clean bill of health, we
left up the quarantine notice until sun, wind, and rain eradi-
cated its message. No sign has ever proved as effective in
keeping away solicitors and sightseers and we have posted
the gamut from "Beware—Unleashed Guard Dogs" to "Great
Danes—Enter At Own Risk." It was particularly useful in dis-
couraging acquaintances *with children* from dropping by un-
announced on weekends.

The *Life* story led indirectly to our learning that it is sometimes best to leave a stone unturned unless you wish to find a
snake.

The charming then-wife of a former Las Vegas property
owner saw the photographs of our house and asked if Eszter
would be interested in transforming theirs. Eszter was told she
could tear down or put up anything she wanted, with one
exception. The owner wished no structural changes in a room
he used each day—the card room. Fair enough; every man
should have a retreat when the remodeling gang moves in.
Eszter was very excited about the prospect of having *carte
blanche* to design, among other things, tiles, fabrics, and a
stained-glass window based on her favorite flower, the poppy.
(The way she pronounces that word, one looks about for a
very small dog.) And the fact that this house was once owned
by her film idol, Gary Cooper, clinched the deal. Eszter had
been expelled from a convent school in Hungary for going
over the wall on three successive evenings to see *Mr. Deeds
Goes to Town*. "That's when I decided to marry him."

Several years ago, a story in the Los Angeles *Times* explained why that card area had been declared off limits. Into the ceiling and walls of the room, the owner had been putting his own creative touches, ones which would bloom greener than poppies of tile and glass. Behind the panels he had secreted the latest in electronic gear and a man with twenty-twenty vision. This all-seeing fellow spent the afternoons looking through peepholes, munching corned beef sandwiches, and signaling the host on how best to cheat his close friends.

The next magazine to show up was *Look*. They wanted a picture story on how a designer cooked and served. It sounded like a pretty silly old-hat idea to both of us; yet the thought that just one of *Look*'s several million readers—namely, Mother —would see the story was too tempting a morsel for Eszter to forsake. When the food editor arrived with *her* menu of how *we* ate, Eszter discovered that vengeance is sour.

The young lady turned out to be the sort of woman Mother always wanted for a daughter-in-law—WASP-waisted and fat-minded. Eszter and the editor met over the kitchen cutting board.

"You're Hungarian, aren't you?"

"I was born in Hungary. I've been an American citizen for fifteen years."

"You Hungarians love chicken paprikas. I know, we've done a lot of stories on ethnic cooking."

"I do not like it. Bruce does not like it. It's far too rich to have more than once a year."

"I've planned it as the main dish of your meal."

"But I'm telling you we very rarely eat it."

"If you've forgotten how, I have my own recipe I'll loan you."

Eszter excused herself and we had a conference in the dog-house, while the editor unpacked several chickens which she had brought in her Vuitton carryall.

"I suppose that's what you call freedom of the press?"

"Eszter, please, she came all the way from New York."

"I know. Beth sent her."

"You said yes. Please."

"Okay, but I'm not baking any 'ethnic'—did you catch that dig?—dessert." Turning to the dogs, she added, "You kids are going to have something new for supper. I'll de-bone it for you."

Back at the chopping block, the two women discussed where the meal should be photographed.

"Where would you normally eat?"

"Right here. We call it our living-kitchen. Guests love it and so do we."

"Being California, I was thinking of someplace outside, maybe the terrace under that red tree."

"At night?"

"No, a luncheon."

"On a hot summer day, paprikas for lunch? I wouldn't serve that to the dogcatcher and he's our worst enemy."

"If it makes a pretty pic, isn't that what counts? Call it editorial license. Incidentally, I am a graduate home economist, you know. University of Indiana, Class of fifty."

From that moment on, all conversation came straight from the freezer section of the refrigerator.

"Miss, I mean, you're not married, are you? Well, my husband, who has been an editor on *Holiday* and *Esquire*, warned me what might happen if we agreed to this story. So it's my own fault. Therefore, I'll do anything you say, *but* we reserve the right after seeing the pictures to say 'nem.' That's Hungarian for 'no.'" And with that the graduate of Budapest's University of Fine Arts, Class of '45, went out to the terrace and set up the most beautiful luncheon table this side of the old Pavillon. She then went back into the study, shut the door, and picked up her creative sedative—an unfinished piece of needle painting. The needle went in and out of the canvas like pins in a voodoo doll. An hour later, the food editor interrupted what I have come to call Eszter's "embroodery" sessions.

"Could you help me pour the sauce off the paprikas?"

1. Eszter comforting Dorka prior to the Dane's thirty hours' labor.

2. Sharing Dorka's burden. A pup is wet-nursed on goat's milk.

3. Nine and a tail of Dorka's litter.

4. Dorka, resting between nursing sessions.

5. It was hard to count them all, impossible to name them.

6. Questionable chaperones. Dorka, Iago (her son) and the Siamese kittens.

7. Brinks in Eszter's hair, a game that alienated a mother-in-law.

8. 1961: An empty black pool surrounded by scrub. 1962: Eszter's hand-painted oasis of delicious guilt.

9. Brink's lifelong problem: How to get out once he got in.

10. Brinks did everything with Eszter—gardening, shopping, sunbathing.

11. Tiffany trying the impossible: To clear the pool of ducks.

12. While waiting for the pool to be cleaned, duck strolls driveway.

13. Ping Pong.

14. Blind Tiffany hears Dr. Sprowl giving Petunia a shot. He was next.

15. One of the rare times Kati was not a loner.

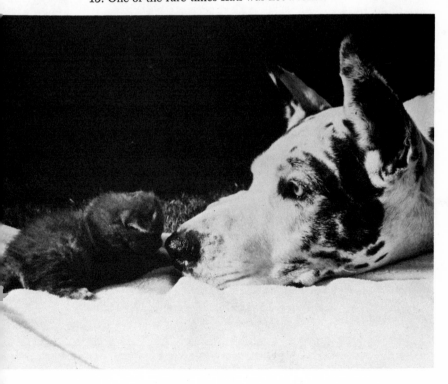

16. Pancake and Petunia before the roof fell in.

"You're joking. That's like eating eggs Benedict without hollandaise."

"I know, but we can't see the chicken. Come on out, you'll get what I mean."

On the terrace, Eszter's colorful table setting was just as she had left it, but the china and wine glasses were strangely empty.

"Where's the food? Where's the photographer?"

"I knew you wouldn't mind"—she was pointing toward the lawn area, some distance away—"I found your fun table and the cabinet with all the glass plates and bowls."

There on the newly seeded lawn stood a glass slab on four spindly legs, the size of an operating table and twice as sterile. It had been, up until this moment, kept out of sight in the garage and used as a storage surface for old newspapers and magazines. Atop this cold monster, the editor had arranged four place settings along with serving dishes containing the various courses, from cold cherry soup (the only item on the menu which was Eszter's) to a strawberry shortcake, the kind that Mother would have made. Aside from napkins and silver, everything was of glass. The photographer lay on his back, taking shots up through the glass table. It was a brilliant idea if *Look* had a big readership among worms.

"Don't you think it's peachy?" I mentally corrected her graduating class to 1940. "The only trouble is, Howard can't focus on the chicken. It's all that sauce at the bottom of the bowl. I'll just wash it off."

We stood by while each piece had a sponge bath and then watched in fascination as our visiting home economist sprayed every leg, thigh, and breast with hair lacquer so that Howard might catch the sparkling, sauceless texture of genuine Hungarian chicken paprikas. For dinner that evening, Dorka and Iago had to settle for some very wilted strawberry shortcake.

When the photographs arrived from New York for our approval, the upside-down table picture closely resembled those pharmaceutical ads in which all sorts of rainbow-colored pills and capsules are spread out on a glass tray. The copy underneath usually says something like: Name your complaint, we have the cure. I wired *Look* that ours was nausea.

The story never ran.

6

A New Friend and the Death of an Old

In spite of the handicap of their names, Petunia and Pancake flourished. When Beth was with us, the kittens were shifted out of her kitchen and put in the laundry room. I spent so much time visiting them, watching and loving their games of who's-afraid-of-a-piece-of-lint and I-can-knock-the-bluing-over-before-you-can, that I suggested to Eszter that they be bedded down in a more convivial area.

"Are you sure? What about your allergy?"

"My eyes didn't run in the laundry room. I think if I just look and don't touch, there won't be any problem. Let's try it in easy stages, anyway."

The two Siamese sensed the conditional nature of my friendship and they went all out to win me over for keeps. They worked as a team in this courtship, each using different tactics of beguilement. Pancake took the aesthetic approach, assuming the guise of a priceless Ming or Egyptian statue. He went from one room to another assessing light conditions, setting, and background before freezing into just the right still life.

Early in the morning Pancake would be ready for me, posing under a pitcher of poppies, head among the blooms, black feet very carefully placed between the yellow and red fallen petals. He could sit there for hours as still and quiet as the dawn, except for his recorded message, in a deep-throated purr, "Aren't I beautiful?" If it was a workday and I had no time for prolonged ohs and ahs, Pancake would follow me to the breakfast table for my coffee and sit down precisely in the center of the newspaper. Only after I had vigorously stroked his ego and his head did he deign to move. Then I was allowed to wash the hairs off my hands with green soap and go back to the paper. Pancake studied and memorized my habits like a zoologist on a field study of the orangutan. Every evening he assumed the same position to welcome me home. He sat, grinning, atop the ice bucket in front of the gin and vermouth bottles.

Pancake still possesses this unfailing instinct to catch my attention by being in the wrong place at the right time. He knows seconds before I that it is time to stop procrastinating and go back to the typewriter. He is lounging in my desk chair when I get to the study. Pushed off, he jumps to the exact center of the typewriter and sits down. That is a doubly difficult spot to shoo him off, since it is an electric machine and he finds its purr very *simpatico*. The television set is also in this room; therefore, Pancake does not have to move very far for his next obstructive act.

When Eszter is doing embroidery and only half-concentrating on an old movie (unless it stars Mr. Cooper), Pancake deposits his sixteen pounds in her yarn basket. But when I turn on the nightly news report anxious to know what is going on outside our tiny little world, he stations himself directly in front of the set. With his back to the screen, his posture and gaze are noble and self-sacrificing as he shields me from the horrors of the day.

While Pancake makes his presence indelible by being the

hair in the camera's eye, Petunia plays the role of the teasing ingenue one can never quite focus upon. She's here, there, everywhere. Independent and gay one minute, misunderstood and tragic the next. She loves her brother but thinks him a terrible square. Her meows are octaves higher than his and full of poor-pitiful-me's.

Petunia's initial moves to capture my heart were calculated to wring it first with pity. Each morning she would sit by her empty food dish crying hunger. The implication was quite clear: Pancake had been doing all the eating and were it not for my refills of tuna and liver she would surely waste away. She did everything but show me her food stamps. When there was a splinter in her foot or a tick on her chest, acquired during a night of gouging on gophers and field mice, Petunia would limp around Eszter and come to me for care and comfort. Early in her acting career, she discovered what a tragic picture she made with one leg caught in her collar. After using up all other ploys for sympathy, she would fall back on this three-legged hobble.

If our more learned friends are correct in saying that majestic, dark-dark-brown Pancake is the sort of fellow the ancient Chinese prized as a palace cat, then lighter-colored Petunia must be a direct descendant of those court ladies who flittered in and out of the king's chamber when the queen was indisposed. Certainly, her technique in our bedroom was very knowing. For it was she who led Pancake in the final campaign which ended in my total capitulation. Their war banner was: "Damn the Allergies."

The Siamese, each working on a different flank, had slowly gained possession of nine tenths of the house. It was at our bedroom door that I drew the line of last defense. One spot had to be itchless, tearless, and sneezeproof. Eszter agreed; but as I vowed never to surrender this last bastion she listened with the cynical air of one who knows that in the cat-owner relationship, cat is master.

The enemy began their siege by scaling the outside walls and scratching on the window screens. After two sleepless nights, we locked them up in the house. That, of course, was exactly what they wanted. The attack could be launched from within with impunity. Only desperate fools would throw them outdoors again, now that it had been demonstrated what a little screen clawing could do. The rest was simple. Like sentries, Pancake and Petunia paced back and forth in front of our locked door, howling at each turn in dissonant counterpoint. When it became clear that I was not going to give in so easily, there was a reassignment of duties based on each cat's talent. The stronger, bigger Pancake spent all his time scraping on the door, while the higher-pitched Petunia howled for surrender.

Eszter went out as my emissary to negotiate a truce. I was willing to give up my clothes closet, bureau, bedside cabinet, even the bath. All I wanted was to keep the bed for ourselves. But it was to be unconditional surrender. Eszter, assuring me that she had not gone over to the other side and trying to find a ray of hope in the peace terms, said, "We'll just get another bottle of green soap and keep it in this bathroom." With that, the occupation forces jogged in, jumped on the bed, and proceeded to rasp my face with kisses of forgiveness.

That evening P & P established rules of eminent domain which prevail to this day. Pancake has the right, while I am reading, to sit on my chest and wedge his head under the book in such a way that the bottom half of each page is illustrated with a very lifelike head of a staring Siamese cat. Petunia, on the other hand, has the choice of climbing up and down the mountain peak of blankets made by my feet or of pulling out the plugs to the electric blanket. Bored with either of these pursuits, she can always go listen to the tinkle of bottles on the bathroom shelves.

When the lights are out, Pancake merely shifts with me and deposits his dead weight in the small of my back, but his sister becomes a sleepwalker with a fixed evening route. After dozing on her two thirds of my pillow, she awakens just as I have managed to fall off to sleep and, walking across my face, wriggles under the sheets between Eszter and me. About four

or five in the morning she surfaces to wash her entire body
and Pancake's. Toilet completed, she settles down on Eszter's
face—cheek to cheek, nose to nose—and sleeps that way until
her pillow wakes up.

In the beginning we thought to circumvent these nocturnal
gambols by giving the cats a bed of their own. The bottom
shelf of a built-in cabinet was put at their disposal. My sweaters were left where they were as a mattress and bath towels
became contour sheets. A lovely lower berth, king size and
snug, with the added luxury of radiant heating from a floor
duct directly below. But only when Pancake and Petunia had
been fighting and wanted to sleep in separate beds did one
of them bother using these quarters.

Now that the Siamese had adjusted to our ways, and as
long as I had become addicted to green soap and skin salves,
Eszter put in a good deal of time checking the cat listings in
the Sunday paper's pet column. She never got quite the right
emanations from any of them. However, the word had been
out for some time that there was an animal patsy on Coldwater Canyon who spoke with a Hungarian accent and went
shopping with a live raccoon boa around her neck.

At least twice a week the phone rang and someone said,
"Are you the lady who . . . ?" There were cries in the night
from just-divorced husbands who claimed, "The dog was in
my half of the community property. I really wanted him, but
right now, he ties me down. I mean, who can swing when he's
holding a leash? You know." Or an ex-wife, ten months after
Reno: "Every time my boyfriend sees my cat he starts to cry
and talk about his former wife. Wouldn't you take her? Once
we get married, I promise I'll pick her up." Then there was
the couple who called—it is always the wife—announcing that
they were moving back to New York City and the apartment
life. Their five-year-old dog hated the idea of leaving California. "He's just mad about flowers and he's the spittin' image
of your Dalmatian in *Life*. We've almost house-trained him."

Eventually we had to request an unlisted telephone number, but before that period of golden silence, we received a

call from a charming woman who was trying to cope with a large litter of Blue Persian kittens. Before she gave any away, the prospective foster parent had to submit to a fitness interview. Would Eszter mind? Not at all. She washed her hair, put some snapshots of our animals in her purse, and drove over to be checked out. I understand the questioning lasted a good half-hour, including tea, and stopped just short of "And what religion are you?"

When Eszter returned I thought for a moment that she had been blackballed, for the cat carrier was empty. But the smile on Eszter's face told me I was wrong and out of her purse came two topaz stones wrapped in a ball of blue-gray fur. It literally fit in the palm of Eszter's hand. "I wanted to take one of her brothers so she wouldn't be lonely, but they'd all been spoken for. What'll we name her?" I was alone in thinking that "Itch" had a nice ring to it. Eszter didn't even bother to say no; she was tracing with her finger the kitten's round head, tiny circular paws, and round belly. "She reminds me of that potty picture of Kati. They're both all circles." On our bathroom wall hangs a picture of Eszter's niece taken, *au naturel,* when she was six months old. And that was the rationale behind the christening of our newest animal.

Kati should have had a sibling to call her own. Perhaps then the Persian would not have become such a loner. At first the Siamese were jealous of this intruder. There was a great deal of hissing and arching of backs. For protection at night we kept her in a conical-shaped fish trap on the floor by our bed. It looked like a bamboo dunce cap. And rather than leave her unguarded when no one was at home, she was deposited in a hanging squirrel cage which held ferns. Once their fur unruffled, Pancake and Petunia resorted to the unkindest punishment of all—the silent treatment. They made it quite clear that as far as they were concerned, Kati was just a ball of dust which had somehow fallen out of the vacuum cleaner bag. As for Dorka and Iago, they loved the little thing and were constantly trying to make bodily contact. Unfortunately, Kati at her heaviest, four and a half pounds, was too fragile for their bone-jarring kisses. Brinks, a loner himself, recognized and respected the signs in another. Theirs was a passing relationship.

When Kati reached the age of consent, she and Eszter paid a visit to Dr. Sprowl. What better cure for loneliness than to have children? The patient, diplomatic doctor wasn't so sure:

"You see, Mrs. Colen, she's very small. We'll have to perform a Caesarean for sure. Knowing how emotionally involved you get with your animals, I'd think twice."

Eszter came home and followed his advice. But while she was debating the pros and cons of allowing Kati to get pregnant, the cat took the matter into her own hands.

Though Kati was a loner, she was not the wandering sort. Every day, after breakfast, Pancake and Petunia would go their separate ways, panhandling around the neighborhood for a saucer of milk or some leftover chicken. Pancake worked the houses below our gate, while his sister paid calls in the opposite direction along Mulholland Drive. I have come to suspect that, like hobos, cats leave secret markings on the gates and back doors of the families who can always be counted on for a generous handout. For in the years ahead, as our cat population skyrocketed, we always received calls from the same neighbors saying so-and-so was in their pantry. Kati was never among the spongers. She knew her own physical limitations and that outside the fence line was an alien world of coyotes, hawks, and—far more dangerous—people and cars. She was in the habit of trailing behind Pancake down the driveway as he went off on his morning rounds, but as soon as they reached the gate, she would turn around and scurry home. In the ten years we shared bed and board together, only once did Kati succumb to the mysterious lure of the outside world. That was the afternoon she and Eszter returned from Dr. Sprowl's.

The object of Kati's curiosity was a huge male cat that had been prowling the hills for the past month, an exceedingly fascinating fellow who was wearing a coat the exact same color as hers. By the time she got close enough to see that it was mutation Persian, and very scraggly at that, it was too late.

Her kittens were delivered courtesy of the Pacific Telephone Company. Rather than go to the expense and bother of a Caesarean, Kati decided to have her children prematurely. I was at the studio when labor began, so for a delivery room assistant Eszter called Dr. Sprowl.

"The first one is stuck, Doctor, what'll I do?"

"Bring the mother to the phone—I mean, is her basket nearby?"

"At my feet."

"All right. Now take the birth in your hand and pull. Hurry, or it will suffocate."

"It won't budge."

"Put the phone down, Mrs. Colen, and use both hands."

That did it. Dr. Spowl went on to talk her through the second and last delivery, a ladylike number of children for such a small cat. Kati was a good and proud mother while her kittens were young; but as soon as they were old enough to fend for themselves, she cut the strings, threw away the apron forever, and went back to her solitary ways. Children were clearly not the answer to her companionship problem, so the breech baby was given to the original Kati and the other to the only woman I know who loves animals as shamelessly as Eszter, Cynthia Lindsay. Stunt girl in *Footlight Parade,* author of a wonderful devilish book on the California Syndrome, *The Natives Are Restless,* and the most compulsive buyer since God ordered one of everything. Antique dealers and scrounge-shop owners around the world have a secret trade expression, "Here comes a Cynnie," meaning a sure customer has entered their premises.

Cynthia had been the ecology-minded, imaginative donor of those five thousand ladybugs and, since it was aphid time, we invited her to come by for the defrosting. She had been canvasing the rock shops that morning. I remember because her loaded station wagon could not make it up the steep driveway and she parked down by the gate. We met her in the orchard with our boxes of dozing friends, like a couple carrying box lunches to a picnic. First, the fruit trees were wetted down so that the ladybugs could have their apéritif before settling down to the feast of work. We opened the boxes. The occupants were beginning to stagger about as they came out of their deep slumber. At the start a teaspoon was used to dollop them over the infested leaves. But they clung to the spoon, slugabeds not quite ready to face the day. We finally used our fingers and blew the bugs off, reverting to the childhood game of making wishes. Out of breath and having guaranteed ourselves a lifetime of good fortune, we wafted the last of the ladybugs to her appointed leaf. Then came the spectator sport of watching to see if these spotted creatures could really be counted on to eat their weight in pests.

Since they were her present, Cynthia felt responsible and moved from tree to tree flicking the bugs closer to the aphids. She need not have bothered. They circled in on the feast more precisely than the Politburo around a caviar buffet. Several days later, the leaves and new buds were scourged of their pestilence. And therein lay our problem. With no more aphids to eat, the ladybugs took off for our neighbors' trees. Given the choice of providing more food for these wonderful balancers of nature or seeing them fly away, we said good-bye. I will admit that I wondered at the time if such a public service was tax deductible.

One evening Brinks, for the second time, failed to show up for the ritual of his raw egg cocktail. I tried to reassure Eszter: "I'm sure he's just visiting one of the neighbors."

"No. He does that much later at night. Something's happened to him."

There was no arguing the first point, for it always was around midnight that we received phone calls reporting that a raccoon was trying to break in or was making fierce faces through the picture window. When we first got Brinks, Eszter visited every house within a mile leaving word that if the occupants saw a raccoon with a red collar not to worry. If the latter was an emotional impossibility, would they please telephone and we would pick him up. Throwing him some pieces of sugar to wash would keep the uninvited guest occupied until we got there. Actually, Eszter always made the pickups accompanied by Iago, knowing how I felt about appearing in public wearing those asbestos gloves.

Periodically throughout that night, we walked along the fence lines calling for Brinks. It was almost dawn when we fell asleep. The last thing Eszter said was, "I know he's dead or hurt. He would have come to us otherwise."

The animal had tried.

In the morning I found Brinks sprawled halfway through the cat door in the kitchen. His hindquarters lay on the stoop outside, one leg smashed in a heavy trap. The pain and exhaustion of dragging himself and the vicious clamp home were pathetically evident. The small body writhed and heaved in spastic plunges at freedom. From his mouth came blowing sounds, whimpers, shrieks. Brinks was too terrified to allow even Eszter within helping range.

We mixed a raw egg with the powder from two phenobarbital capsules and placed this palliative on the tile floor by his head. Slowly, he licked it up. In time he was too drowsy to lift his head. I removed the blood-smeared trap and we bundled him in a blanket for the trip to the vet. Iago had been standing by all the time, wanting to help but wary of the raccoon's bared teeth. As soon as the phenobarbital took effect, he began licking and cleaning his friend's mangled leg.

We caught Dr. Sprowl at one of those rare moments when summer vacations, early lunch hours, and a high surf at Malibu had decimated his staff. Looking around for an aide, the doctor noticed my curds-and-whey pallor and impressed Eszter into service to administer the oxygen. Halfway through the operation to remove the mashed toes on Brinks's trapped foot, the animal's heart came to a stop. Eszter's tears were silent, her voice a whisper to herself, "It's my fault. Only a goddamn egotist would try to civilize a thing that's wild." Sprowl grabbed the oxygen cone and turned the valve to high. As Brinks started breathing again, Eszter wiped away her tears and looked at him with the sort of adoration which only Richard Chamberlain received when "Dr. Kildare" topped the Nielsen ratings.

Until the stitches came out and the bandages came off, Brinks had to be kept indoors. The kitchen seemed the ideal barracoon for his period of confinement. It had washable surfaces and enough human traffic so that he would not be lonely. We barricaded the cat door, inside and out, with cushions and metal porch furniture. All ground-level cupboards were securely fastened with wire. During the week of Brinks's recuperation, the cats climbed the social ladder coming and going through the front door, which was left ajar. So did the summer flies, the Danes, and one disoriented skunk. The dogs chased the wanderer from the premises; although, before leaving, the skunk paused to spray them and the living room with his special forget-me-not scent. It was a very bad week.

By the time Brinks was well enough to be let loose, the inventory of kitchen damage included:

1 de-strawed broom
1 broken sugar bowl with screw top
3 electric plugs severed from appliance cords
4 cushions from outdoor furniture minus foam rubber stuffing
5 cupboard doors severely scarred by attempts to jimmy with tooth-sharp tool
30 feet of chewed and paintless baseboard
1 princess phone desperately in need of corrective facial surgery

Three weeks later, Brinks was back in his kitchen convalescent home. This time he had been shot through the other paw. We knew, and he knew, that someone out there was bent on killing him. Long after the bullet wound in his foot had healed we kept him shut up. But the time soon came when we could no longer smother our conscience. The doors and window frames in the kitchen still bear the gnaw marks of Brinks's disdain for the domesticated life. We let him loose. The sounds of pure joy which he made as he headed for the wild fields told us that we were at least right, if not sanguine. For weeks thereafter, Brinks came out of nowhere when he heard the ice trays cracking; and after his egg and a gambol with Eszter, he was off again. Because of the injured paws his scramble was more lopsided than usual, but he was still very fast.

One Sunday morning I was awakened by muffled murmurs. Eszter had her head buried in the pillow. "About an hour ago, I heard a shot. I loved him so much."

"I'm sure it was just a car backfiring on Mulholland."

When Brinks did not return that evening or the next, I whistled in the dark some more. "Please don't worry so soon. He's probably found some wild raccoons and decided to go back in the hills to live with them for a while." But Eszter was not taking such easy comfort.

"We made him half-tame. They'd never accept him now. He's an outcast. No, Brinks is dead."

The following Wednesday in the mail, which I picked up at the gate each evening, was a small box. There was no return address on the plain brown wrapper. The contents were more obscene than any pornographic book. Inside lay Brinks's red collar and identification tag. Before entering the house, I dropped the killer's trophies into the garbage can and said nothing. Eszter, reading this, will learn for the first time of my deception eight years ago. We had learned the hard way that no amount of love compensates for the wrong of domesticating a wild creature.

The best cure for forgetting one disaster is to become mired in another. Eszter's reluctant entrance into the world of high fashion took our minds off Brinks's "disappearance." She was pushed into the business by two gentlemen whose respect for her talents as a designer could be matched only by their total ignorance of the garment industry. For Charles

Lederer and myself a cutting room was where motion picture film is pieced together and if something was "done on the bias," you looked around for a prejudiced person. Charlie and I backed our faith and ignorance with $84,000, nine tenths of which was his. E.H. INC. was born.

Nine months later, one of the most beautiful high-fashion collections (see New York *Times,* Los Angeles *Times, Women's Wear Daily* for unbiased superlatives) of the late sixties was unveiled. If future fashion historians are in any doubt about the exact moment when the American woman decided that haute couture was dead and "sewing up your own little thing" was in, let me pinpoint the time. To the month, day, and hour it was when eight models stepped out on our terrace and paraded through the garden in fifty-four sophisticated dresses, coats, and suits, not one of which could sell for less than four hundred dollars and many of which would have to cost three times that. The department store buyers stood up to applaud; but when the time came to write up orders, their hands were in their pockets. They knew, before anyone else, that the affluent society had gone underground and taken its money with it. The era of blue jeans and kitsch was upon us.

The residual effects of the fashion holocaust were similar to those of an earthquake: for many months we experienced aftershocks. The first, and highest on the Richter scale, was expected. We were broke. Our savings were tied up in bolts of cloth and dress dummies. The latter, though perfect size tens, shrunk to eights in the damp garage. Since our newly acquired Mexican couple were understandably not very excited about being paid in needles, pins, buttons, or thread, we had to tell them the bad news. It was not easy. They loved the guest room and the doghouse, for it was there that Maria cooked her husband's noonday meal and served him in the shade of our special peach tree.

This was a young Babcock, found dying of neglect in a remote corner of the property. It was transplanted to give the doghouse shade and nursed back to bursting, blooming life.

Now, each summer as though in gratitude for our attentions, the tree bore the sweetiest, juiciest fruit we had ever tasted. This was our prize. Maria understood very little that we said, but she sensed this pride.

We had paid the couple to the end of the month. A week short of that date, they left with their few belongings in the middle of the night. Feeling very small and petty, I nevertheless looked through the house to see if anything was missing. Eszter caught me taking inventory. "Who ever heard of anybody stealing stainless steel silver?" I stopped and we went out to the doghouse to say good morning to Dorka and Iago. Every peach, ripe or not, had been stripped from the Babcock. I still feel the shame of that moment, the have-nots getting back at the haves.

Seventh Avenue may have lost a brilliant designer, but we gained two white rabbits. In the E.H. collection were four angora blazers in red, blue, yellow, beige, and white stripes. On the off-chance that the buyers and press might be looking at legs when these evening sport coats went by, Eszter decided to have each of the models carry a tiny angora rabbit. When the show was over and the last of the overly convivial buyers drove off with fuzz on their lapels, I rushed the rabbits back to the pet shop. The owner greeted me at the door with a "Closed" sign in his hand. "Nope, no returns on rabbits."

"You can keep the money. Just take them back, please."

"Not on your life."

"At least swap me this female for another male?"

"Sorry, mister. Easter's way gone and I'm gettin' out of the bunny business. I never thought I'd get rid of those, until you came along. They're a real mess, you'll see."

"Mess" is a clean word for what they were. Fiasco and Never Again—it was painfully easy finding names for them —were chicken-wired in under the Babcock. I was quite proud of the location I had chosen. The dogs would have a sideshow right outside their front door and the tree would receive a daily dose of nitrogen. Best of all, the trunk of the peach tree would save me the labor of sinking a fourth post-hole for the hutch.

It took forty-eight hours for the dogs to become disen-chanted with the white fluffy things which just stood around twitching their noses and looking nervous, and the same pe-riod of time for all the flies in the neighborhood to discover that I was experimenting in instant fertilization. Worst of all, we discovered that rabbits will turn down a bushel basket of carrots and greens if there is a single piece of wood within nibbling reach. The peach tree was being chewed to the quick. While I was trying to solve these problems, Eszter noticed a more catastrophic one: Never Again was big and lush and itching to multiply. Out came the cat carrier and in went Fiasco, the male rabbit. It was Sprowl time again.

When I returned with the deflated Fiasco, Eszter was there in the center of the driveway looking happier than I had seen her since the rise and sudden fall of E.H. INC. Beside her stood our once-a-week cleaning woman, Hortense. All three hundred pounds of the heir apparent to Maria were jiggling with joy. Eszter gave me a now-don't-blow-it look.

"I told Hortense that you just didn't have time to care for the rabbits and that as much as we adore them we have to give them away."

To Eszter's Vivien Leigh, Hortense played Hattie McDaniel: "Ah just adores those big white cottony things, Mr. Colen, and Ah'll love 'em as much as you does. Please say I can have 'em."

I was never a good actor, but on this occasion only Leslie Howard could have matched the humble sincerity of my sim-ple reply, "They're yours, Hortense, God bless you."

Every Wednesday, Hortense entertained us with stories about Fiasco and Never Again. There were so many verbatim reports of what the rabbits said to her in strictest confidence that I had the feeling we were sitting through weekly mat-inees of *Harvey*. Then, one week, no show. Perhaps Hortense was sick. Since Eszter did the telephoning that evening to find out, all I heard was her side of the conversation. It went something like this:

"Hi, Hortense. Are you okay? . . . I can't hear you, Hortense. Is it your throat? . . . Oh, that's good, we thought you were sick. What happened today? . . . Hortense, why aren't you talking? . . . How are the rabbits? . . . WHAT! . . . That's impossible. You were right there when Mr. Colen brought him back from the vet. . . . How many? . . . Oh my God . . . Hortense, listen, of course it's a dirty trick, but I'd never do anything like that. . . . Twelve you say? . . . Hortense, wait a minute. . . . Hortense? . . . Hortense? . . . Operator, I've been disconnected. . . . Oh, thank you."

All future Wednesday-afternoon performances were canceled due to the absence of the star. There was absolutely no way of convincing Hortense that we had not knowingly, and with malice aforethought, given her fourteen rabbits when she wanted only two. To double-check, we had taken out a calendar and counted back thirty-two days, the gestation period for most rabbits. According to our calculations, Never Again's twelve children were conceived about the time I was warming up the car to shepherd Fiasco to Dr. Sprowl for his vasectomy.

7

A Gray Fedora

By now we had made so many trips to the Brentwood Pet Clinic that the Danes went straight to the huge rotary index while their case histories were pulled. The sound of the file drum clicking around was like a lollipop to a child getting its first haircut. The dogs drooled with pleasure. One day while I was waiting in the reception room and the head nurse was Kleenexing Iago's saliva from her desk, an attendant came out to talk with me. The young man thought Iago the most beautiful black Dane he had ever seen, including his own black bitch, who also had some Canadian Blue in her background. Would I allow him to breed the two? Instead of a stud fee, we could have the pick of the litter.

It seemed a harmless way to alleviate Iago's incestuous frustrations and I agreed, upon two conditions: One, he did not have to pay a stud fee, but under no circumstances would we take one of the puppies. This was to be a purely altruistic, therapeutic encounter. Second, the breeding was to take place off our premises. Iago would have to be bused back and forth from the meeting. Nor did we want to hear any of the details. Our pool-deck memories would last a lifetime. Per my orders, the assignation went off on schedule and *in absentia*. The only indication we had of how the meeting had gone was the worldly-wise look in Iago's brown eyes and an added degree of pride in the tilt of his head. The incident was forgotten and we concentrated on a more important matter: how to escape from paradise.

For over three years we had worked full weeks and long hours to create a special, private world of our own. We loved what was happening to the land and never regretted the day-in, day-out chores or the nursery bills; but the dreamers had finally become prisoners of their dream. Only during the brief time Maria was with us did we dare leave the animals and the gardens unattended for a weekend in San Francisco. Before tedium and confinement ruined it all, another escape was mandatory. Easier demanded than delivered.

Boarding out five animals was prohibitive and calling for the traditional help of all trapped parents—having Mother stay with the children—was not very realistic in our case. What we needed was a house sitter, preferably an independently wealthy one who would be insulted at the thought of recompense, a person to whom we could entrust the wildlife, vertebral and non. Henry Isaacs was that man and friend. A perennial bachelor, there was no question of a wife bathing in Eszter's perfume or checking out the linen closet. As a dedicated gardener, he would see to it that pots, plants, and shrubs were watered twice a day during the heat waves of summer even if it did take over two hours of hosing and regulating sprinklers. The house itself would probably look better than when we had left it, for among Henry's other virtues are tidiness and thrift. He is the only man I ever heard of who washes out his pipe cleaners to be used another time. Best of all, Henry loved the animals, especially Iago. In fact, his affection for the big black Dane was at times slightly excessive. During his first stint as house sitter, Henry gave a luncheon party for Iago, where the guest of honor was dressed in one of my sweaters. Now, *that* we never did.

Ten leisurely days of touring California's spectacular coastline, from Santa Barbara to Mendocino, was all the break we needed. Driving home through the blue gate, what had seemed just a short time ago a prison farm was now the loveliest place in the world. We were ready, even anxious, to get back to work. The dogs were a bit heavier, Henry several pounds lighter. He talked about taking a few days' rest in Carmel. As our good friend got into his car to drive off, he remembered something. "Just before you got back, a Harry called. He said just to tell you they're beautiful. I'm sorry I forget his last name." Harry was the owner of the dog to whom Iago had been bred.

It would be straining the reader's patience and intelligence to make a lengthy mystery of what happened next. Eszter went "just to look." We agreed that I should stay at home as insurance against her bringing back one of Iago's children: it takes two to commit sins which a single person would only dream of. Eszter brought home, on approval, a small gray fedora. The color was not what I had in mind, the nap went every which way, and I was not too sure about the size; but it was the most lovable Great Dane puppy I ever saw. And I had seen seventeen.

My first audience with Iago's son was almost our last. I had been down on the pool deck giving Dorka and Iago their monthly bath, when Eszter arrived with the gray package cradled against her jacket. Iago was eager for a closer look. Exerting the weight of his parental rights, he jumped up, forcing Eszter to open her arms. The puppy did a splashing one-and-a-half gainer and plummeted to the bottom of the pool with the speed of a sounding lead. Surprised and outraged by this inhospitable reception, the puppy must have forgotten to breathe, for he bobbed right back up to see who had pushed him in. We wrung out Tiffany—he was silver blue, not the purist's steel blue—and took him to the doghouse, where he was tucked in between the warm flanks of his father and grandmother.

Tiffany proved impervious to the traumas of childhood. After the flower beds, the pool became his favorite stamping ground. On hot days while Dorka and Iago sat on their haunches in the shallow end of the pool watching the bees and birds take pollen and insects from the surrounding trees (they looked very much like two elderly people dunking at the seashore) Tiffany would paddle about endlessly. His unique swimming style involved going no place in particular and getting there as slowly as possible. Half the time his paws never broke water and he moved them just enough to stay afloat. Only the tip of his nose, eyes, and ears were periscoped above surface. When Eszter and I stood at either side of the pool playing keep-away with Dorka and Iago, their heir cruised the deep end shagging misthrown balls. It was quieter there and he got the ball as often as they did, only with far less exertion. I would not say that Tiff was lazy, just the most adjusted of dogs. A good thing, too, for in later years his patience and good nature were cruelly tested.

This seems an appropriate moment to mention a running controversy which splutters between us and our guests. Many of them actually question the propriety of dogs and people sharing the same swimming hole. I quickly point out that aside from the fact that the Danes have second proprietary rights, they, like all dogs, show certain hygienic restraints which children and adults do not. I ask if they have read the latest figures on how many thousands of tons of human excrement are pumped daily into the swimming waters of the California coast. And for those who rhapsodize about the purity of a mountain stream or a woodsy pond, I question whether they have counted the number of cows or paper mills upstream or how many beavers, deer, ducks, or bears may have visited the pond and bathed in their absence. Being a polite host, I never mention the fact that fish do something besides eating, sleeping, and spawning. Chlorine notwithstanding, most people are still lost in the egocentric predicament. Only one of our friends, Luther Davis, has ever thought to ask, "Do you think the Danes would mind if I went in?"

When a very special animal comes your way, the impulse to name it after a very special person is hard to resist. Tiffany's initial labeling by color was merely an introduction to his proper and legal name, the one registered with the American Kennel Club: Tiffany Alan Jackson of Dorkadane. "Come here, Tiffany Alan Jackson of Dorkadane" echoing through the canyons sounded quite idiotic; besides, one such call and we were breathless. For everyday usage, it was "Tiffany" or "Tiff."

Unfortunately, we met Alan Jackson only a few years before his death. Already, the first hacks and rasps of throat cancer could be heard in his voice. He and his wife, Phyllis, had come out from New York to spend Christmas with Cynthia and she brought them up to see the animals, the flowers, the house, and, incidentally, the owners. Cynthia is such a satisfying admirer of the place, long ago we awarded her sole rights to the tour concession. At fifty cents a head, half for us, half for her, we thought Cynthia would be more than happy, but she is constantly complaining that the guide uniform we provided is baggy and the megaphone too small.

The moment Alan pried his six-six frame from the car, the Danes smelled a lover of big dogs who had been deprived of their company by the restrictions of apartment living. They welcomed him en masse. While Dorka licked his face and neck, Iago concentrated on Alan's pants pockets, front and rear, on the off chance that this nice-smelling visitor might be carrying a concealed cookie or two. (Iago was not far off, each dog received a Life Saver.) Pint-size Tiffany had to content himself with saying hello to Alan's knees and shaking the tall gentleman's shoelaces.

Alan had to be so tall to hold all the wonderful things he was. This gentle, witty man had that rare quality—two parts childishness, three parts sophistication—of making something extra special out of every occasion, no matter how trivial or brief. A dreary journey to Palm Springs became a flight across the Sahara with Rommel in pursuit; a drive to the liquor store and we became Prohibition rumrunners sneaking a load through a heavy fog off the New Jersey coast. A man who knew sadness, he blocked its shadow from those around him.

The way he said good morning guaranteed that you were going to have just that. As those who greatly prize life, Alan was a taker. But he took by giving.

Alan was not supposed to drink or smoke. He did, nevertheless, when he thought that Phyllis's back was turned. Of course he was not fooling her and he knew it; but it was a game to be played, a pretense which helped mask the inevitable. Our house was ideally suited for these deceptions. While I made a pitcher of cocktails in the kitchen, Alan smoked and stood guard at the Dutch door, which afforded an oblique view, through a living room window, of the rest of the company. At these moments, our assembled guests were all wondering when we would be finished with our secret operation so that they might come out and replenish their drinks. Cocktails in hand, Alan and I called the Danes and sneaked around back to the doghouse, where the five of us settled down to an hour or two of man-to-man conversation. Being the only female in the group, Dorka only spoke when spoken to. I have never felt any guilt about aiding and abetting in these behind-the-barn goings on; for should I ever be in the same critical stage, I hope someone will join me in the doghouse for a toast, a cigarette, and the foolish nothings which mean everything.

Tiffany was almost two when word came that Alan was soon to die. For company and love we sent him a twelve-by-fourteen color photograph of the gray Dane looking his usual discombobulated self. In the matte below the picture was inserted Tiffany Alan Jackson's official name certificate from the Kennel Club. When Phyllis next came to California she brought me a gold taxi whistle which had been Alan's. I went to the front door and blew it and the three Danes came bounding up the hill, Tiffany Alan in the lead. That night their kibble was mixed with some of my tears.

For someone who professed little interest in founding a Great Dane dynasty, I showed an inordinate fondness for this newest member of the Dorkadane clan. Until Tiffany was big enough to push me off the couch we took naps together;

17. Tiffany, about a year before he went blind.

18. Picture of Tiffany sent Alan Jackson before the latter's death.

19. A pause during the 35,040 woman hours' labor.

20. "Please turn on the faucet."

21. "That's enough."

22. What-a-Puss with blossoms from the Babcock peach.

23. The dead California oak before it became a bougainvillaea umbrella.

24. Petunia traverses Dorka's spine.

25. What-a-Puss.

26. After dripping faucets, Whatta likes the fridge best.

27. Cigar box furnished by B.C. for E.C., Christmas 1969.

28. Ping Pong, "a purring garbage disposal of life's pressures."

29. Ping Pong and Whatta disregard the spatterware bowl they broke.

30. G.B.S.—one up, one down.

31. G.B.S., "the master of conspicuous consumption," finds another toy.

and though feeding the animals from the dinner table was a household no, scraps had a ouija board way of jiggling off my plate when the gray one was around. We went everywhere together and it was not long before I found myself introducing Tiffany to guests before Eszter. Dorka and Iago received merely passing attention. One evening we had a showdown, probably the quietest of our marriage, for Eszter simply told a story, a true one, and it marked the end of my playing favorites.

"Back in New York, before we knew each other, I once designed the interiors of a big brownstone for a very wealthy divorcée. The woman had a Pekingese and a six-year-old daughter. It seemed that every time I went to the house to go over plans, the child was downstairs playing by herself, while the mother was upstairs stretched out on her bedroom chaise fondling the Peke with one hand and holding the phone with the other. It was hard to decide which was more disgusting, the drooling she did over the phone or over the dog.

"One day when I arrived with some new designs, the little girl followed me upstairs and stood at the bedroom door while I worked with her mother. The child didn't say a word; her eyes remained fixed upon the mother petting the Pekingese. The steady stare made the woman nervous. 'What's wrong, darling? Don't just stand there like an imbecile, say something.'

"There was no answer.

"'You don't want Miss Haraszty to think you're a rude little girl, do you? Come in and talk to us.'

"The child neither moved nor spoke.

"'Now tell Mother what's going wrong or I'm going to punish you. What are you thinking?'

"Very quietly, as the child turned to go back and play by herself, she said, 'I wish I were a dog.'"

8

Arthur Godfrey Is a Good Scarecrow

The flower gardens were blooming, the orchard was bearing —I will never understand why lime trees insist on producing fruit only during winter, the non-gin-and-tonic months—and the dog and cat population was a three-to-three standoff; but something was missing. Eszter thought she knew the answer. "What we need is a vegetable garden. Every time we eat a scallion it's a vote for Reagan." Those were the days when Cesar Chavez was struggling to win a fair deal for his farm workers, and picket lines ringed the local supermarkets. Thank God the dog meat people were not on strike or my social conscience would have been sorely tested, but I certainly was not going to cross the line for a head of lettuce.

Across the lawn, outside our bedroom door, seemed an ideal spot. The area received full sun from nine to five and it was far enough from the house so that tomato poles and plastic sheeting for covering the strawberry beds would not be an eyesore, yet close enough for us to keep an eye on. We were wrong about the latter.

On a bright Saturday morning I went out to prepare the simple ten-by-thirty-foot bed. At dusk on Sunday, I laid down my pick, shovel, spade, hoe, rake, and body. I had struck the richest vein of adobe north of Santa Fe. The following weekend three trips were made to Stevens's Nursery for Nitro-humus and topsoil to replace the adobe, and four to the brick-yard for mortar and cement blocks to shore up a slight earth slide which had occurred when the adobe was hacked out. The local car wash insisted on charging dump truck rates to clean our Ford convertible.

As though to make up for its unfriendly soil, Southern California has a delightfully short germinating period. A week or so after planting the seeds, radishes, scallions, and lettuce were pushing aside my imported soil with absolutely no regard for the fact that it cost roughly fifty cents a square foot. Eszter and I played the age-old game of all gardeners and children: Who First Saw What Come Up. Since I was the early riser in the family, one would imagine that most of the discoveries were mine; but Eszter has green eyes as well as thumbs, and besides, as she pointed out, I kept making false claims. "You're cheating again. We didn't plant spinach. That's a weed."

The birds had no such difficulty in botanical identification. With the greatest of ease they separated the vegetable seedlings from crab grass and dandelions. They had joined our game and defeated us with ease and were taking out their winnings in green shoots. We would never taste the fruits of our labor unless something was done at once.

That there were so many nibbling bluejays and sparrows is partially my fault. The previous Christmas I surprised myself and Eszter by making a birdhouse. I was quite proud of the architecture, rather Neo-Zhivago in feeling, and put it up on a red pole within view of the bedroom so that Eszter could claim bird watching as an additional excuse for not getting up earlier. The house was fully rented within days and there was a standing line waiting for vacancies. The landlord's thoughtfulness in providing a backyard vegetable patch proved as popular with the birds as the local delicatessen is with a city bachelor.

I covered my beautiful structure with a green garbage-can liner; but the birds must have thought that their house was merely being fumigated, for they bivouacked in nearby trees waiting for the Grand Reopening. Next, out came one of the $84,000 dress dummies from the garage. Eszter made a scarecrow. It wore knee-high boots, a mini skirt, a dazzling sequin jacket, and an Aussie's campaign hat with dangling ribbons which darted about in the faintest breeze. Too bad birds cannot afford to shop in Bergdorf's, Bonwit's, and Bullock's, for they flocked to admire Eszter's creation.

Pancake, Petunia, and Kati joined forces, for once, trying to help us out. And for the first few days their sneak attacks threw the enemy into confusion, but then the bluejays countered with quick swoops and pecks on the head. The cats turned pacifists. As for the dogs, standing in the sun all day scaring off creatures no bigger than their ears was no sport at all. Their attitude was clear: If you wanted bird dogs, you should have raised setters.

We were about to surrender and do without salad until Mr. Chavez won, when I remembered the booming cannons which periodically frighten the crows from corn and wheat fields in the Midwest. Our neighbors would never stand for such thunderous salutes, but certainly a low-playing portable radio could not be considered noise pollution? The hour of D day had to be just before dawn, when the birds started their foraging. Eszter was protected by a supply of earplugs left over from the remodeling furor. So that some sharp-eyed robin would not recognize my sound machine as one of those gadgets he had seen by the millions from Canada to Mexico, I camouflaged the radio under a bushel basket in the center of the garden. For the first week it cleared the area of birds faster than Lawrence Welk at a rock festival. The expense of replacing batteries was outweighed by the euphoria of victory.

But I was thinking human, not bird, and soon they found

my FM selections the ideal music to eat by. Not even the morning news scared them off. I tried talk shows and Walter Cronkite's political commentaries. These proved a source of boredom and they ate twice as much in frustration. Only Arthur Godfrey was totally effective. There was something about that homespun voice which sent them away for hours. Thanks to Godfrey, CBS, and Lipton Tea, we somehow managed to nurse our crops past the baby stage. At that point, the birds found the greens too *al dente* for their palate. However, the texture and size were exactly what the gophers were looking for.

Over the years, one of our favorite pastimes has been garden watching. This lengthy session, in contrast to the frequent shorter peeks we took each day, fills our Sunday mornings. With coffee in one hand, a cigarette in the other, we walk about the property inspecting plants, trees, and flowers, seeing what another week of sun and water has brought. On these trips of discovery, it is imperative that both of our hands are occupied, otherwise we end up pruning and weeding and Sunday becomes just another day. It was at the end of such a tour that we stood surveying the vegetable garden. The kohlrabi had reached maturity and we were anticipating having it raw as part of a luncheon *crudité*. Eszter nudged me and pointed. A choice kohlrabi was slowly sinking into the earth. It was like watching a sidewalk elevator's gradual disappearance. The leaves of the plant folded together, in broken umbrella fashion, and vanished. A second or two later, the next kohlrabi started a similar slow-motion descent. My silent fascination gave way to a roar of anger. The elevator stopped just short of the ground floor. Too late, the first reconnaissance gopher had located the booty and was off to tell his friends there was a lot more where that came from.

In years ahead when archaeologists excavate the Stalag 17s of Europe they will find about as many tunnels as undermined the vegetable garden in the next few weeks. The only difference in the network of burrows was one of direction: The prisoners of World War II wanted out; our gophers wanted in.

Both groups of tunnelers showed amazing ingenuity and perseverance. We came to have a grudging admiration for our underground thieves. To reach the salad bed they had to dig down under a four-foot cement-block retaining wall and then up again. When we placed arsenic in their holes, they either nosed the pellets back to the surface or they made new, hairpin channels around the poison. Someone suggested drowning them with a hose; that was merely wasting water on China. The cats were no help either. They much preferred dining out on neighbors' rodents. As for the Danes? Again we were confusing breeds. This was a job for terriers.

The one thing that worked were steel traps; and because Eszter's hands and stomach were too weak to set and unload the heavy springs, the unpleasant job was mine. Reminding myself that these were destructive, vermin-carrying creatures did not help a bit. They were clever, hard-working, remarkable engineers. There was even something cute about their buck teeth and balloon cheeks. Fortunately, word got around very quickly that the Colens' vegetable patch was boobytrapped and the gopher colony moved off to safer ground.

With the birds in transit there was no one left to pick the green worms from the tomato vines, squash leaf hoppers on the pepper bushes, flick blister beetles off the squash, snare the flea hoppers dancing on the cucumbers, or stifle the spittle bugs slopping all over the strawberry plants. No one, that is, except Eszter. She had a more delicate touch, better eyesight, and after all, I had done my bit in the gopher pogrom. But neither of us could handle the aphids (white, green, red, and black) which suddenly blanketed the garden. No matter what it said on the bottle about being safe for human consumption, we did not want to use insecticides. The ladybug cure was out. It was far too expensive to ship in workers who were always looking over the fence at greener aphids. Native Californians—anyone who can pronounce *camino real* without making it sound like a square dance—advised planting garlic between the rows of vegetables. We did not have to waste time or hope on this old wives' tale, for right before our eyes was proof to the contrary. Between two rows of artichoke plants a bed of garlic was already in full flourish. So were the swarms of aphids on the former, so intent upon eating they had no time to breathe the aromas from next door. The insects wormed their way right down to the heart of the artichokes, leaving us no alternative but to let the globes go to bloom. Their beautiful thistle flowers almost took our thoughts off of how good they would have tasted steamed in consommé and dipped in garlic butter broth.

Eddie Albert, a consummate gardener and a devout ecologist in the days when that word came up only at spelling bees, touted marigolds as an insect repellent. Contrary to his role in "Green Acres," he was right. A border of these pungent-smelling yellow and orange flowers around the vegetable garden provided an olfactory barrier against some of the flying pests. The majority were not so sensitive. Only the birds, graciously forgiving my sneaky behavior with the radio and returning to eat meaty bugs instead of tender greens, saved enough of the crops so that we were to know the pleasures of harvesting and eating your own.

Cesar Chavez's victory garden taught us three basic lessons about future plantings:

1) No matter how few tomato vines one plants, no matter how populous or greedy the green worms, no two people, their friends, neighbors or enemies, can eat the seasonal output. As a matter of fact, we found that our dinner invitations were declined in inverse proportion to the size of the harvest. Only True Blue Cynthia would tell us the reason why.

"When you two arrive for an evening, it's like checking in a shipment of CARE packages. Nobody, outside of Clarence C. Birdseye, ever has that much refrigerator space. And look, Eszter dear, while we're on the subject, what about those bloomin' armfuls of 'puppies,' too? I mean, with a house full of guests, who's got time to hunt up five or six vases for those damn beautiful things?"

2) Eszter: "I vill not put down anything. Canning is for

mothers. Vut ve can't eat, ve vaste." She relented when it came to pickling the cucumbers, because they looked so wonderful curing in a huge glass jar on the terrace table.

3) There is an Italian salad, *ruchetta,* which the birds, gophers, and insects avoided as though the Mafia were pushing it. The herb grows like a weed, seeds itself, and has a marvelously fresh, piquant taste. I imagine that someday more Americans will discover and prize this very special green; and when they do, of course, then the birds and bugs will move in. Before that time, hopefully, our place will be a sea of *ruchetta.*

As the years slid by, we were so intent upon keeping ahead of nature, the mortgage, and property taxes (they have quadrupled in eleven years) that we never thought we were getting older. Only the sight of acacia and pine trees tripling in size, or the fact that I now had to use a pole to reach oranges and lemons which had once been within arm's reach, reminded us that seven years had come and gone since we started putting all our eggs in one basket. However, it was the Danes—cats never seem to age—who most clearly marked the passage of time.

Dorka was beginning to act like a senior citizen at Sun City. Things had to be just right. If her food was either too cold or too hot, she would stand about guarding the bowl from Iago and Tiffany until it reached room temperature. Her teeth could only handle Milkbones when they were broken into bite-size pieces, and every evening at bedtime a geriatric pill was popped down her throat before we covered her with a blanket as protection against the damp night air. She spent more and more time baking her bones in the hot sun, only stepping into the pool for a few seconds to cool off. Iago and Tiffany found it harder and harder getting the old girl to join their games. Dorka wanted peace and quiet; that was what the generation gap was for. Her greatest treat was joining Eszter on the study sofa at embroidery time. She made herself as small and quiet as possible, hiding her head under a pillow or behind Eszter's back, for fear someone might discover the black and white bolster and send it out to play.

While not yet ready for a retirement community, Iago's muzzle was turning snow white along with his eyebrows, and those soft brown eyes seemed deeper and sadder as the lower lids began to droop. In a way, Tiffany was the most dramatic calendar of passing years. It seemed just a few days before yesterday that I had held a velvet-soft bundle of dangling ears in one hand. Now, it took two arms and a great deal of grunting to stand on the bathroom scale with him in my arms. He weighed in at a good trim 130 pounds.

At first we attributed Tiffany's constant habit of bumping into things and people to the exuberance and rudeness of youth. All three dogs had been trained to watch their step in the house. We were very proud of their manners. In seven years the only breakage was an occasional glass left at wagging tail level on the coffee table. Tiffany shattered that lovely record. In quick succession he knocked over several stools, toppled a piece of sculpture from its plinth, and sat down on what had been an eighteenth-century yarn winder. He was barred from the house until he passed through this destructive phase. The one which followed was far more disturbing. Tiffany became passive, almost timid. He outlounged Dorka, and his only pleasure seemed to be in eating. Instead of racing Dorka and Iago up the driveway with the morning paper, he quietly took up the rear. When they were all invited into the house, he stood aside, the last to enter.

One morning there was a nasty gash on Tiffany's forehead. The dogs played hard among themselves, but never that rough. While cleaning his cut and powdering it with antibiotics, I discovered the cause of the wound. The disinfectant stung. Tiffany wriggled from my grasp and ran out of the doghouse. In his escape he misjudged the opening of the sliding door and cut himself again, in the same spot, on the metal door handle.

Tiffany was blind.

Dr. Sprowl confirmed what we should have known weeks

before when all that furniture and pottery were flying about. The Dane had cataracts in both eyes. Had Tiffany been an old dog, perhaps we would have accepted the fact, taken him and our sorrow home, and done the best we could to make the dog's remaining days safe and comfortable ones. But Tiff had just reached the midway point in the average life expectancy of a Great Dane—nine years. Dr. Sprowl said that there was a veterinary surgeon in the San Fernando Valley who was having great success in the removal of cataracts. Did I want him to make an appointment? I did.

Then came that moment of guilt known to all animal lovers. The operation would cost $250 for each eye, the sort of figure one thinks thrice about; although that was not the point, for Eszter and I would have done without something or sold a painting for Tiffany's operation. Could we, though, spend $250 to heal a dog when the same sum would pay for a ghetto child's summer vacation or, a better parallel, help defray the expenses of a blind person's Seeing Eye dog? The rational answer is no; the gut response, yes. The compromise? To do both. I took Tiffany to the surgeon, stopping at the post office on the way to mail a conscience check to the Seeing Eye foundation.

The operation on Tiff's right eye was not a success. Several weeks after the bandages were removed, the dog seemed to see moving objects and we were hopeful that as the scars healed, the vision in that one eye would continue to improve. But being able to distinguish between dark and light was as far as he ever got. And then, suddenly, that faint glimmer vanished. Tiffany was totally blind again.

We did not have to face, another time, the moral and economic questions of whether to operate on the left eye. Tiffany adjusted himself to a dark world with amazing skill and speed. Where once he had seen the difference between friend and stranger, he now separated the two by the sound of their cars and some not so discreet nosing. Women held down their skirts, men shuffled sideways and hopped about a lot. The jangle of the car keys being taken off the kitchen shelf, not the way I dressed, told him it was shopping time and he ran to the car, hoping for a ride. We are not one of those couples who constantly shift about furniture to give their lives variety, so Tiffany knew the floor plan, but if in doubt he followed in his father's footsteps. When a new lounge was placed on the pool deck or some planting tubs added to the terrace, he was taken over and introduced to them. I went about the doghouse with a roll of adhesive and pieces of foam rubber, taping protective bumpers on all the sharp edges and rough corners. It looked like a well-padded gym. Dorka and Iago were clearly aware of Tiffany's handicap. Without coddling him, both were discreetly protective. They stopped playing their old game of let's-snitch-his-bone-when-he-isn't-looking, and neither would settle down for the night if Tiffany was off wandering about the property by himself. The one place where the blind Dane got into any trouble was across the driveway and over the wooden bridge, where strange things were happening to Eszter's studio.

9

The Reluctant Landlords

Shana Alexander had moved on from *Life* to become editor of *McCall's*. Remembering the wall-to-wall embroidery and the fence-to-fence flowers, she paid Eszter a double tribute by commissioning a series of needlepainting kits for *McCall's* readers and by making her the magazine's garden consultant. We decided to do something besides sleeping on the financial cushion which came from these assignments.

"For once in our lives, let's be smart about money. You know, I know, and the nursery people know we're going to put those *McCall's* checks right back into the place. Right? Since it's inevitable, let's fool ourselves—remember your mother—and spend it on something which will bring us an income."

I quickly made it clear that we were not going to start a Great Dane kennel or a catachresis or whatever a cat kennel is called, nor did I plan to expand the vegetable garden so that we could sell *ruchetta* at a little stand on Coldwater Canyon.

"Don't be silly. We remodel the studio. Have a rental unit. I've always wanted to be a landlord."

"You mean landlady."

"No I don't. They always walk around with curlers, an apron on, and a broom in their hand. Landlords sit behind big oak tables, dropping the rent money into a slot."

I liked that vision. The jangled nerves of another remodeling brouhaha would not be too hard to take if it were followed by the soothing jingle of silver. That we were not going to be exactly absentee landlords and would eventually have to share the property with a stranger was a problem we brushed aside with the sawdust for the moment. But unconsciously, we were already protecting ourselves from "that other person" becoming a couple. The blueprints for the new house—again, their existence solely in Eszter's head presented a few problems when the building inspector came around—provided for a cesspool just big enough for one.

We skimped in no other area. The one-room studio rambled on until it included a bedroom, study, living room, kitchen, and one and a half baths. Because of the sloping nature of the land, the additions seemed to float out and rest among the surrounding acacia and silver eucalyptus. When the framing was up, it had the look and feeling of a child's super-deluxe tree house.

During the four months it took Fred to build the place, with only the help of his sons, garden watching took second place to the fun of house inspection. Every evening, cocktails were taken out to these wall-less rooms. We loved the nestlike quality and started to hate the idea that anyone other than ourselves or close friends would ever live in what we were calling the guest cottage ("rental house" sounded far too commercial for such a romantic place).

The finished house was even more nearly perfect than the one we had imagined during those hours of sitting on sawhorses and nail kegs, looking up through bare beams at leaves and sky for a roof. And so, in our enthusiasm, it was inevitable that we should violate the First Principle of all successful landlords: "Don't furnish as you would, furnish as they do." By "they" the masters of depreciation and amortization have in mind a color-blind, tasteless blob who thinks hospital green the most soothing of colors and a mirror framed in an old dray-horse collar the ultimate in décor. The same we-know-the-public thinking governs the choice of coffee table: a ship hatch entombed in resin; lamp base: coffee grinder; and doormat: "Drop Dead." Against the advice of such experts, we did it according to our taste, as though we were going to move in tomorrow and leave the big house to the animals. The net result: We found ourselves many thousands of dollars over budget. So, as attached as we were to this home not far away from home, the original plan of renting it had to be pursued. Our reluctance, and hope for a last-minute reprieve, were reflected in the terms we asked: a *very* high rent, tenant to pay all utilities, a year's lease, and no sublet clause.

Two days before the *Home* section of the Los Angeles *Times* was to feature a cover story on the guest house, I ran an ad in *Daily Variety,* a trade paper for the entertainment industry. *Variety* and its competitor, *The Hollywood Reporter,* are dedicated to the journalistic principle that hearsay and gossip make worthier reading than the facts. Since the truth about the motion picture and television business is mighty grim, they may have a point. In any event, every Producer, Director, Writer, and actor in town sweetens his morning coffee with these fantasy sheets. Divorce, separation, and roller-coaster incomes being occupational hazards of these four professions, the trade papers prosper from each Friday's jam-packed advertisement section of houses for sale and places to rent.

Our listing was sandwiched between a "Forced Sale" Bel Air mansion, placed on the market to settle community property, and a Malibu beach pad sublet headed "Rated R." It called attention to the pictures of the guest house in Sunday's newspaper and made it discouragingly clear that we would consider only a quiet, sober, very single person. The *Variety* clerk who took the ad over the phone suggested that the first line should read: Wealthy Priest Wanted.

The phone rang just as we were getting to sleep Saturday

evening. Eszter contained her annoyance until the conversation was over and then asked me, "Who's uncivilized enough to call at a quarter to twelve?"

"A woman caught the ad and then bought the bulldog edition of the *Times* to see the pictures. She apologized for calling so late, but to quote, 'Frankly, I must have that heavenly house.'"

"The word 'heavenly' means she's either twelve or menopausal."

"I didn't ask her age. She promised to bring a check for the first and last months' rent plus whatever we want for security, if we'll just not answer any more calls until she gets here with the money. Sounded perfectly nice."

"What kind of a person telephones at this hour?"

"Somebody who really loves the house and doesn't want to lose it. That's a good sign."

"I don't know. As long as we've gone this far, I guess we have to at least see her. I've heard women tenants are always asking you to change light bulbs and call for help at the first drop of a leaky faucet."

As I fell off to sleep, I heard Eszter murmur hopefully, "Maybe her check will spring." She meant bounce, of course.

Bright and too early the next morning, the woman drove up with a gentleman. Eszter was wrong about her age. She seemed like a perfectly normal, fragmented woman of forty. Nor was there anything particularly ominous about her companion, unless you were picky about appropriate clothing for house hunting. He was dressed sloppy-casual in Abercrombie & Fitch's most expensive sailing gear, although the nearest yawl was an hour farther west. Clearly, here was a gentleman who had discovered the freedom of California living and canceled his Brooks Brothers charge account after decades of good standing. They introduced themselves as Mr. and Mrs. Swift and, without even looking in the direction of the guest house, handed me a check. Matching their alacrity, I handed it back, although it must be admitted that my palm did twitch ever so slightly in the latter exchange. I explained why the ad had very clearly stated one person only. Mrs. Swift interrupted this Sunday-morning lecture on cesspool capacity to say that the lease could be made out for one. Except on very rare occasions she would be living alone.

Mr. Swift had businesses in New York, Mexico, and Hawaii which kept him away most of the time. And when he was in California, the gentleman claimed, he could get a good night's rest only if he was rocked to sleep on his boat, parked in the Marina del Rey. Frankly—Mrs. Swift used that word a great deal—she wanted the house because she was sick and tired of rolling around on planes or boats. Her husband promised to retire in a year and then they would buy their own place. "And, frankly, I don't mean a houseboat. But Tommy can have his own water bed."

Mr. Swift kept nodding agreement to all she said and shifting from one foot to another. I attributed this balancing motion to long years of standing on the deck before the wheel and it gave credence to his wife's story. Later, we learned, among other things, that Mr. Swift took his first vodka when the sun peaked over the boom. I asked if Eszter and I could be excused for a moment while we digested their offer.

We went straight to the doghouse, where Iago and Tiffany were trying to coax Dorka into going out to play. Lately the old girl wanted to do nothing but sleep until noon. Perhaps if I had not locked up the three of them when the gate bell rang, the Swifts might have been scared off and we would not have been sitting there, with Dorka between us, debating what to do. Eszter asked me what I thought.

"The story's just kooky enough to be true. Anyway, we'd be protected by the signed lease saying 'one only.'"

"Sounds like a happy marriage. I feel sort of sorry for her. Him, too, but the way he rolls from one foot to the other makes me seasick."

"Don't. Please. We're about to become landlords, not marriage counselors. What have we got to lose?" The answer to that question was our innocence.

However, it all started well. The Swifts kept to their bargain with us and themselves. Tommy rarely put in an appearance. And we found to our great relief that the guest house was so well hidden only the mailman knew that another party shared the property.

In with the second month's rent check was a note from Mrs. Swift, inquiring if she might have her two Pekingese stay with her. They had been hidden away at a dog motel while she got up the courage to ask. My immediate reaction was negative, but I knew there was no chance of winning. What I find ugly and sneezy-looking about their squashed-in faces is exactly the quality which endears the breed to Eszter. For form sake, I kept saying no until Caramel and Taffy showed up and then the three Danes joined me in actively loathing the silly creatures. Against my better judgment, I saved the asthmatics from being chewed apart as they jumped out of Mrs. Swift's car. Even this bloody beginning failed to sway Eszter. The thought that there would be two more animals about, and Pekingese at that, which we did not have to take care of was too great a temptation. Eszter did make Mrs. Swift promise, though, to keep Caramel and Taffy in the house until her husband fenced in a spot for them.

Tommy was a long time in coming and when he did arrive he had difficulty remembering which house was his, so I knew no postholes would be dug on that visit. More weeks passed and the Pekingese remained cooped up, snarling out the bedroom window at the Great Danes, who were playing a waiting game on their side of the bridge. Looking at dogs through a smudged window, fifty feet away, was not exactly what Eszter had had in mind when she voted for their being allowed to stay. She was increasingly concerned not only about the imprisoned Pekes but what the house must be like now that it had become a twenty-four-hour kennel. She phoned Mrs. Swift and suggested that a fence company could solve the problem in an hour. No fencing man showed up, but each morning a few orange crates and boards left over from the construction of the house popped their ugly heads out of the ground. It was a makeshift, useless barrier.

This time I called. Starting off with Robert Frost's line about good fences making good neighbors, I moved on to less poetic literature and quoted the lease, "No dogs allowed." Then it all came gushing out, like the dirty water from an overheated car.

"Mr. Colen, I'm not going to spend one penny of my money on this place. That's his responsibility."

"But they are your dogs, Mrs. Swift."

"If I had a proper husband, I wouldn't need two dogs for companionship."

"Well, where's Mr. Swift?"

"Back in New York with his wife and children. For the past five years, he's been swearing he'd get a divorce. It's liquor that keeps them together, you know. Frankly, Mr. Colen, I've about had it."

Our first venture as landlords had turned into a shoddy soap opera and both of us felt sad and slightly tarnished. I went to take a shower. Halfway through, I heard screams for help and the barks of the Danes in fighting voice. Barefooted and with only a towel knotted around my waist, I ran outside and straight for the guest house. Eszter had been doing her daily fifty laps when the screaming started. Holding a towel around her nakedness, she came running up from the pool. We met at the bridge.

Mrs. Swift, high-heeled and overdressed, stood on the bank leading to the wash. She was engaged in the seemingly impossible—doing five things at once: hopping up and down like a pogo stick, wringing her hands, wailing, pointing to the gully, and crying, "They're killing my babies, my babies." I looked under the bridge and, indeed, Iago and Tiffany seemed to have just that in mind. Each had his own Pekingese by the scruff of the neck, kneading the yapping things and tossing them up in the air with all the *élan* of a good pizza maker. Dorka stood by, ready to catch any misses.

Down in the soggy bottom of the gully, struggling to sep-

arate the foursome, my towel slipped off; but I was not completely naked. In place of terry, there was blood, mud, saliva,
and hairy swatches of Caramel and Taffy. Mrs. Swift fell
suddenly quiet. She stared with all the attention given mud
wrestlers in a Hamburg waterfront dive. Eszter covered my
embarrassment. As I handed up Caramel, she took off her
towel and wrapped it around the shivering, blood-soaked
animal. Now Mrs. Swift was the odd one. Looking neither
here nor there, she asked, "What should I do?"

"Go call Dr. Sprowl. His number's in the phone book. Brentwood. Explain what happened and tell him you'll be right
there with two dogs who need immediate attention. He's
closed on Sunday, but he'll go down to his office for an
emergency." When she returned from making the telephone
call, Eszter and I were back in towels.

Only in retrospect is there anything funny about that dog-
fight. At the time, we were both very frightened. Mrs. Swift
got splashed with the spill-over of our trembling anxiety.
"How could you let something like this happen, after all our
warnings?"

"I know, Mrs. Colen, but you don't have to yell at me.
Taffy had to tinkle. I was on the phone trying to find Tommy
and I just let them out without thinking."

Eszter, in an even louder voice, "You are a totally irresponsi-
ble, selfish woman. You don't deserve dogs and certainly not
this house." She gestured toward the ramshackled assortment of crates, outdoor cushions, bits of clothesline, and an
empty Smirnoff case posing as a fence, "You've turned the
place into a pigsty."

Not surprisingly, those turned out to be our final words
with Mrs. Swift. As we helped her into the car with Caramel
and Taffy, the only sound was the feeble yaps of the Pekingese. Later, Eszter called Dr. Sprowl and found that he had
spent a good part of his Sunday afternoon darning and stitch-
ing, but both dogs would be fine. Monday morning, a mile-
long Bekins van stripped the branches, right and left, off the
acacia trees as it plowed up the driveway to take away five

small cartons of Miss Swift's belongings. Tuesday morning we received a letter from the elusive Mr. Swift saying that he was terminating the lease because "Your Great Danes are an ever present danger to my wife's safety and peace of mind." I wanted to write back saying that Tiffany and Iago had never been in New York, but Eszter was so pleased at having the lease broken she made me promise to drop the matter.

10

To Please and Love

For several months we had been carefully avoiding any discussion of a fact which was very obvious to us both: Dorka's life was slowly but surely coming to an end. There were no specific ailments, merely the symptom and sign of mortality, a gradual lessening of life and spirit. Dorka was twelve. In Great Dane circles, that entitled her to the respect and care due the very old.

While we did not talk about the inevitable, each did little things to make the lovely lady's remaining days comfortable, happy ones. When either of us took a nap on the study couch, Dorka was allowed to squeeze in. Actually, she was the only one who got any rest on those occasions; for in her old age, the Dane had a recurrent dream that called for a great deal of running and twitching. The couch shook like a weight-reducing machine in high gear. If the evenings were chilly, she was allowed back on the foot of the bed, an indulgence banned since the days of her pregnancy. The general disintegration was most evident in her wobbly legs. To prevent side splits, fore and aft, on the slippery stretches of oak and tile floor, the hotel towels were taken out again and put down as gangplanks. A walk from the kitchen to the bedroom became a fluffy white reminder of our travels from the El Camino in Mexico City to Budapest's Gellért. We were foolish, we were emotionally indulgent; but these were hardly great sins if they made happy a gentle being who for more than a decade wanted only to please and comfort and share our love.

Dorka was eating less and less, so in place of quantity we tempted her daily with what had formerly been once-a-month treats: ice cream served at room temperature, fresh marrow bones big enough for her tongue to explore, and strawberries. Dorka loved strawberries almost as much as cracked crab. But the *pièce de résistance* had always been liver scraps sautéed in the leftover drippings from a roast chicken or broiler. One night I found Eszter sitting on the mat in the doghouse, hand-feeding Dorka these favorite morsels. The Dane would take only two, those simply to please Eszter. That no more were consumed was taken as a sign by Eszter and I heard her whisper, "If you die, Dorka, I'll kill you." Both of them looked like they were crying.

A week or so later it happened.

I had put the Danes's breakfast bowls in their stands, lined up in order of age outside the doghouse, and called for them to come and get it. No customer raced out the door. Inside, I found Tiffany and Iago crouched down on either side of Dorka, licking the matriarch's closed eyes and limp ears. Her breathing was heavy and slow and it was only with great effort that she managed to lift her head in my direction. Coaxing, cajoling, and gentle prods were all futile in getting the animal to rise. I was no longer interested in having her eat; it was a question of reaching Dr. Sprowl's while she was still alive. Trying to lift her, my arms and back buckled under the 150 pounds of dead weight. Eszter was asleep. I prayed she would stay that way until Dorka was in the hospital. Using a blanket under the Dane's stomach as a sling, and walking straddle-legged, the two of us finally made it to the car.

Along the way, Iago and Tiffany kept pushing and poking. They were not playing games. The proddings were those of concerned children wanting to know what was the matter. With the car door open, I placed the animal's forelegs on the front seat and pushed in her hindquarters with my hands and shoulder.

The freeway would have been the fastest route, but my concentration was not to be trusted for that kind of driving. I was right; for while going the slower, safer way, I found myself petting Dorka's head, which rested on my thigh, and talking to her about happy yesterdays. To passing motorists, I must have looked like one of those young women drivers who seem constantly to be talking to themselves. They are not, of course. There is usually a two-year-old sprawled on the floor or seat, chewing the strap on Mother's handbag.

"Remember the last time you were pushed up like that, Dorkie?" I was referring to our train trip West ten years before, which also happened to be the honeymoon of the just married Colens.

Dorka had slept with us from New York's Grand Central Station to Union Station in Los Angeles.

Well, not quite with us. We had a roomette and while she occupied the upper berth, Eszter and I shared the lower. Actually, it was the largest compartment on the train, the one film stars of the thirties and forties lounged about in when their contracts had just been renewed for five years at five thousand dollars per week. Those Hollywood dream days had long passed, along with the popularity of rail travel. Now, an extra fifteen dollars bought you the star suite. Poor, generous Hubbell had agreed to pay our moving expenses to California. Considering that this involved the cost of shipping the contents of our two bachelor apartments clear across the nation, it is not surprising that the sumptuous accommodations went unquestioned, particularly when they avoided another chit for shipping Dorka separately. An alternative which

Eszter wouldn't allow anyway. "Just ask Hubbell how he'd like to be cooped up in a crate for seventy-two hours." Somehow, I forgot to pass on the query.

As for the New York Central going along with this *ménage à trois,* by the time they discovered the conspiracy, the train was pulling out of Grand Central. My secretary had come to see us off, carrying a bottle of champagne in one hand and leading a rather familiar black-and-white-spotted Dane with the other. When the conductor called all aboard, the former had been consumed and the latter was hiding under the lower berth. After supper, the porter arrived to make up our beds. Eszter had her purse open—ready, willing, and waiting to buy a little kindness. He took one look at our stowaway, who had poked her head out to check the visitor, smiled, and asked, "Which berth gets the two pillows?"

He refused a tip, saying, "Don't you worry, missus. I'll take a dog to a cross-country drunk any day."

Once the upper had been organized, Eszter climbed up and called, "Come on, Dorka. Bedtime." And with a push here and a pat there, up the ladder she went. We were still congratulating ourselves on the ease of it all, when the porter announced that the train was about to pull into its first milk stop, one of those brief halts when I was to take Dorka for a walk. Up went the ladder, but Dorka would not budge. We had forgotten a basic weakness of all children, two-legged and four. They have very little trouble learning to climb stairs, but the descent is one of the last things they master. And a ladder is only for graduate students.

Eszter pushed and I pulled. Dorka would not budge. The train was slowing to a halt. I need not labor the point that, since there are no such things as Dane diapers, it was imperative that we not miss one of these infrequent stops.

Dorka would not budge.

Ester said, "Vun more time. Vun, two, tree." "Tree" coincided with the lurching stop of the train. Down came Dorka, ladder and all.

Practice did not make perfect. We went through the same tug of war three or four times every twenty-four hours; since, during the day, after Dorka had had her fill of treeless prairies and stockyards containing a depressing number of black-and-white-spotted heifers, she climbed the ladder and took a nap. As we pulled into Los Angeles, Dorka got even for the days of asking a lady to do what no lady can do gracefully: climb down from an upper berth.

Our bags were packed and stacked in the corridor outside the open compartment door, when we started the last debunking. This time, set for the siege, Dorka had buried herself under the sheets and blankets. She was playing dead. Eszter managed the unveiling, but the dog remained deaf to all entreaties. Passing remarks from departing passengers as to how to handle the situation were not helping matters. One little old lady accused us of deliberate cruelty to a poor defenseless animal and threatened to notify the ASPCA. I gave up tugging and switched to swearing. Eszter yelled down,

"Stop calling her that. You know Dorka isn't a boy. Stop and think."

I stopped and thought and rang for the porter. While I pulled Dorka, he pulled me. In the midst of our third heave-ho, Dorka decided to accept defeat gracefully. She leaped into my arms. The porter cushioned my backward fall and I softened Dorka's.

From our landfall out in the aisle, I looked up at Eszter and discovered a most unwifely trait. I had married a woman who went into contortions of hysterical laughter at other people's pratfalls. Little wonder Laurel and Hardy are Hungary's favorite comedians.

As we drove into Dr. Sprowl's parking lot, Dorka opened her eyes, looked around, and promptly shut them again. Over the years, unlike Iago and Tiffany, this had been the moment when she always started to shiver a little. I am sure that this reaction was not because the dog associated pain with white coats, stainless steel tables, or with the color spectrum of pills in huge glass jars. More likely, she simply dreaded a repetition of those times when, because of a serious ailment, we had to leave her overnight. There must be truth to the theory that dogs have no sense of time, no instinct to know that a future follows the now. When left at the doctor's, loving Dorka must have felt she would never see us again. This morning, for the first time, she did not tremble.

An attendant helped me carry Dorka in and put her down on the floor of the operating room. While the examination was going on, her head rested in my lap. Dr. Sprowl put away his stethoscope.

"Well, the only nice thing I can say, Mr. Colen, is that she's in absolutely no pain. Her heart is going and I'm afraid, just like with humans, we can't do anything about that. We can keep her comfortable and feed her intravenously, but the end is here. I'm really sorry. If it's any help, were she my dog I'd put her to sleep."

I said, "Not yet," and used his phone to tell the office not to expect me. I had left a note on the worktable in the doghouse: "Dorka doesn't seem well. I've taken her to the vet. I'm sure it's not serious." Before Eszter read it and called Dr. Sprowl for an explanation, I had to tell her the truth, myself.

An hour before, thinking of the inevitable had been postponed with happy memories of coming West with Dorka. No such mental dodge was possible on the drive home to let Eszter know there would be no more Dorka. Trying to find the words which would soften the blow and lessen the pain was what I had to think about. Eszter loved our animals equally, but her attachment to Dorka was a very special one born of loneliness and welded by mutual need.

When Eszter had been a single woman in New York, Dorka was the someone else who was always there in an empty apartment when the parties were over, when the goodnights had been said. They went everywhere together. Eszter's studio-apartment was on East Nineteenth Street, her design clients' in the Fifties and Sixties. Between business appointments, shopping and errands, the two girls walked a good five miles a day. Once her companion had been trained to "sit and stay" and mind her manners, Eszter went on a scouting trip of New York's restaurants, finding out which hat-check girls were willing to share their cubicle and double up with Dorka while her mistress dined. She came back with a list Craig Claiborne could not fault. Due to certain rumored culinary eccentricities, no Chinese spots were canvassed.

My favorite on the list was Lüchow's. It turned out that this famous old New York restaurant got Dorka's top award, too. The owner, Jan Mitchell, captivated by the Dane's great elegance and ladylike bearing, allowed her to sit in a corner near the front door of the Bar Room, within sight of the booth where Eszter ate. If you stop to think of the number of poodle owners in New York who would have given their latest Pucci for such a place of honor, you begin to understand this Dane's irresistible charm. And unlike many members of her sex, Dorka's charms were not turned off and on. Everyone got the same where-have-you-been-all-my-life treatment. It was her scrambled-gene look. Harlequin Danes absorbed a great deal of albino blood in the steps which led to their domino appearance, and their eyes are a record of that journey. They are as varied in color as a ten-cent-store bag of agates. Dorka's left eye was dark brown; the right, pale pale blue. The one for business, the other for be-witching.

While Eszter dined, Dorka stretched out in her place of honor, head cradled between her front paws, eyes alert to each new customer like a good maître d'. The Lüchow regulars, who dropped by for a nightly stein or two or three, greeted her as one of their cronies. But they were careful not to jeopardize Dorka's status and stuck to the house rule: No Petting, No Feeding. The Bar Room waiters made up for the second prohibition by always presenting Eszter with a fare-well Dorka-bag stuffed with leftovers of *sauerbraten, wiener schnitzel,* venison steak, and every known variety of *wurst.* Dorka's preference for Lüchow's was easily understood.

Friends soon adjusted to the fact that everywhere that Eszter went the Dane was bound to follow. Weekend invitations were extended in the plural. And when Eszter took her yearly summer vacation at Wellfleet, on Cape Cod, it was Dorka who carried the oyster bucket or swam by her side across Great Pond. I once asked if boyfriends had not sometimes objected to the ever present Dane. "No, but twice she took a dislike to fellows. She was right both times."

All in all, Eszter and Dorka's life together had the continuity and memories of a personal diary kept daily for twelve years. Today's date in such a journal would have been March 19, 1969.

The half-hour trip back from the vet produced nothing but a brain mushy with platitudes. As there is no avoiding death, there is no honest substitute for the word itself. I realized that the only thing I could say was simply, "Dorka is dying." Driving through the blue gate, I saw Eszter walking in the daisy field. By the droop of her shoulders and from the way she was looking at everything, yet seeing nothing, I knew I did not have to say anything. Her eyes were swollen and red. There had been tears, but there were none now. We silently embraced until Iago and Tiffany, who had run down to see if Dorka was back, wedged us apart as though they might find her hiding between our legs. Eszter asked, "Do you have a cigarette?" If smoking is ever really banned, mankind will have to devise another ritual that aids procrastination, that bridges silences.

"Is she in pain?"

"No."

"I've been walking around, visiting all the spots we went together. She's really as much a part of this place as we are. And I decided we should let Dorkie die while she can still remember the beautiful sounds, the smells, the shapes of life. What do you think?"

It took a minute to get my voice under control. "I think you're right."

"But, please, I have to say goodbye to her."

That afternoon, Eszter sat on the kennel bedding beside Dorka and repeated over and over all the words and phrases of praise the dog had heard and loved through the years: "Good Dorka," "Beautiful Dorka," "Nice Dorka." I left her for a while to go tell Dr. Sprowl we wanted the dog cremated. When I went back, I found Eszter kissing Dorka on the forehead and saying, "Go to sleep, sweet Dorkie. See you in the morning." She had tucked the animal in with a blanket brought from home.

To this day there is the latent knowledge that something gentle and lovely is missing from our lives. But for the first few months, Dorka's death was ever present. It took me days to stop soaking three bowls of kibble instead of two. I found myself repeatedly calling Dorka when I meant to summon one of the other dogs and, each evening, I often waited to shut the doghouse door because the third Dane was missing. Iago and Tiffany were just as distraught. They showed no interest in food and spent hour after hour standing on the terrace, heads pointed in the direction of the gate. Only the arrival of a car stirred them out of their lethargy for a few moments as they raced to give the vehicle a thorough inspection. They were sure Dorka would come back.

A week after Dorka's death, they ran to check out a United Parcel truck. I could not think what the package was unless Eszter had ordered a two-year supply of checkbooks. The return label read: "Sun Valley Crematory." I tried very hard to dismiss my immediate thoughts of certain passages in Waugh's *The Loved One.*

Something was needed to lift the dark shadow hanging over our lives. An ill wind and my own stupidity provided that something. The distraction was a bit more violent than was really necessary.

It was late spring, that time of year when Southern Californians note a doubling in their water bills. The rainy season is over. The hot Santa Ana winds whistle through the canyons, playing counterpoint to the wail of fire engines on their way to kindled brush. It was past midnight when a noise loud enough to awaken even me made Eszter drop her mystery book. "What was that?"

"A branch on the roof. The wind must have knocked it off the oak. Go back to sleep."

"Can't you see I'm reading?"

"No. I'm sleeping," and in a second I was.

Stumbling toward the coffeepot the following dawn, I found I had been 100 per cent correct about the source of the previous evening's crash, only 10 per cent right about the cause. It was not an ordinary limb which had fallen but a main branch—twenty-four inches in diameter—of the dead live California oak. It lay across the skylight. The bougainvillea that had once encased its bark was cascading through the broken glass along with the first rain of the dry season. The oak floor never had such a shiny patina as then, glistening beneath a half-inch of water. Until the skylight was covered, Eszter could do nothing but admire the floor, so I let her sleep.

Throughout my youth, one of Beth's cheerier warnings had been, "Never leave the house without clean socks and clean linen. If you're in an accident, they may have to cut off your clothes." With this rain, I hardly expected to meet a knife-carrying doctor on the roof and so I dressed accordingly: a pair of knee-high soccer socks which had been aging in my rubber boots since the last storm; over my mini flannel pajama top went a gym sweat suit, and for a final protective coating, I stuffed myself into an oilskin southwester, complete with nose-level hood. In this ratcatcher attire, I took a sheet of heavy plastic and the extension ladder from the garage and climbed to the roof.

An inch or so of wood still held one end of the huge limb to the trunk of the tree. The other end rested on the skylight casement. By lifting the latter portion an inch or so, the plastic could be slipped under and stretched across the six-by-eight-foot hole. Standing between the log and the peak of the roof and straining with both arms proved futile. I would have to use my knee as a wedge as well and to do that I had to move below the log. I remember thinking as I looked down at the brick terrace that it was not the safest of sites; but from this new position, I had a half-inch of success. One more heave would do it. It did it. The log broke away from the trunk and with the edge of the roof as a fulcrum it cast me in a beautiful forty-foot arc to the terrace below.

Just three months before, the resident designer had decided to soften the look of all the brick under the oak by sinking a three-foot-wide flower bed in the center of the terrace. My parabolic flight ended in the center of that soft runway, slicker-shrouded head resting a few poppies and ranunculuses away from the brick border. A split second later, the catapulting limb settled down across my chest.

The pelting rain brought me back to consciousness. Like the balloons in a comic strip, our hills vibrated with my calls for H-E-L-P!!X!!! I have never quite determined whether it is a good mystery book or a bad one that enables Eszter to sleep most soundly. If I knew which she had read the night before my fall, this vexing problem would be solved. All sorts of variations on the cry for help brought none. Only loyal Iago and Tiffany came to see what all the screaming was about. It was a great sacrifice on their part, for both dogs hate the rain. Never having seen me napping under a log in a flower bed, a territory they knew was off limits for them, they could not think of what to do except lick the rain off my face and bark. *That* woke Eszter. A minute later she was standing over me. Looking at her, I realized for the first time what I must look like. Here I had executed one of the most consummate pratfalls since the Keystone Kops; yet there was not a crinkle of a smile upon her face. Gray as her soaked white negligee, she was about to faint. I quickly reported that, though pinned down, I could wiggle my arms and legs. They did not hurt. But a very strange thing was going on inside my chest. It felt as if some Lilliputian was splitting kindling wood in that cavity and then burning it. Trying the impossible, to lift those several hundred board feet of oak timber, Eszter slipped and joined me in the muddy flower bed. She got up crying with frustration and fear. "What shall I do?"

"Call the Fire Department."

Eszter returned, planting a Marimekko umbrella in the ground over my head. She almost smiled. "They told me to tell you not to move."

Iago and Tiffany decided that flower beds were obviously not sacred today and joined me under the mushroom canopy. A few minutes later, their hi-fi rendition of sirens heralded the arrival of the Fire Department. It was at this point that the fire in my chest must have spilled over into certain cranial areas for, according to Eszter, I carried on a most unlikely conversation with the gentlemen in yellow. Unfortunately, her word has to be taken, since I have no memory of what transpired until they deposited me in the ambulance.

Once the limb had been dragged aside, a kindly fireman is reported to have noted, "You're sopping wet. Get some blankets, Charlie."

"Please don't touch my clothes. I'm not dressed."

"Now don't you worry, we'll have you out of here in a split second."

"Eszter, please. They're going to tear off my pants."

"Ma'am, don't worry. He's in shock."

"Please, Eszter. There's a hole in my sock. And I don't have any underwear on."

"Charlie, we better hurry."

They did. That Sunday morning, after twelve years, I finally found a legitimate reason for the existence of freeways: They offer the quickest way to a hospital.

They wheeled me into an X-ray room. A nurse of the new

militant breed sounded off. "My name is Clarissa Slausson. Your doctor [Koblin, not Sprowl] just telephoned with instructions. He wants a complete set of pics, head to toe. Ready?"

My reflex to salute was stifled. I was still swathed in L.A.F.D blankets. "Do you have to undress me?"

"It's the customary procedure, Mr. Collins. Ever take a picture through a blanket?"

"My name is Colen."

"Oh, like the large intestine."

She started with my boots. Trying to pull them off stoked the fire in my chest, so out came a pair of scissors the size of a five-pound lobster claw and equally ominous. Next, Clarissa went to work on the gym suit, cutting each leg from cuff to waist. Holding up the dripping remnants so I could feel them on my face as well as see them, she asked if I wished to save the outfit. I shut my eyes in answer. When I opened them again, Clarissa was standing at the foot of the rack, holding one athletic sock at arm's length with a pair of surgical forceps. "Didn't your mother ever tell you not to go out with holes in your socks?"

Dismiss the nature of his profession and Robert Koblin is a very nice man. He keeps bills and small talk to a minimum. When Clarissa had finished with her fun and trundled me to my room, Bob was there. "You'll be fine. You're very lucky, just broke a few ribs. They'll be taking some more X rays during the day."

"Why?"

"The machine seems to be out of whack. Some of the plates were very cloudy."

Eszter came by at five with a large picnic basket containing a shaker of martinis and enough canapés to allow me the pleasure of saying, "No, thank you" when the hospital dinner was brought around. And under a checked napkin, she had smuggled in Kati for a visit. The Persian took one sniff of the antiseptic surroundings and crawled under the sheets for a little human warmth. At alcohol rubdown time, the nurse cross-examined me re the evidence of gray and blue flocking on the bedding. I shrugged bewilderment and pantomimed that it hurt my ribs too much to talk. The nurse countered by not missing a spot in her application of alcohol.

On his morning rounds, Koblin stopped by. He borrowed my ashtray and, after snubbing out his cigarette, pulled a negative from a large brown envelope. "What do you see?"

"Nothing. It's all snowy."

"Precisely. The X-ray machine wasn't on the fritz, you are. Under that cloud someplace are what's left of your lungs. How much do you smoke a day?"

"Three packs."

"You're going to have to cut that down to none. I know it's hard, I can't do it, but you have to."

"What if I can't?"

"Then, please, try and pay my bill as soon as you can. Sometimes it takes years for estates to be settled."

I was Editor at Large for *McCall's* at the time and although my magazine associates in New York covered the bedside table with messages of condolence, it was quite clear that they all thought falling off a roof was just about the funniest thing they ever heard of. Their laughter secretly bothered me until I stopped to think of the more violent forms of mayhem common to that city. Humor, among other things, is relative and regional. Of course flying off a roof would seem a lark compared to strolling through Central Park after dark or having dinner in a little neighborhood Italian restaurant.

Clarissa and the other nurses showed great thoughtfulness in arranging for my rapid release from the hospital so that I might recuperate at home. As I slowly made my way through the house on that first day home, it was obvious that Bob Koblin had spread the warning word. Every ashtray and cigarette box had vanished. Eszter muttered something about there being too much silver to clean. Like the wife of an alcoholic, her life was hell until my splintered ribs stopped poking me and I could go back to work. Eszter found herself so busy catering to my nicotine-withdrawal symptoms—

roaring irritability and a ravenous appetite—that the only time she had to think of Dorka was while hiding in the garden, sneaking a cigarette.

Yet another distraction, of a far more painful nature, kept our thoughts in limbo. We decided to raise a few chickens.

11

The Great Chicken Wars

It all started out in such a friendly way. Who would have thought that the end would bring threats of shooting, screams of agony?

Our neighbors to the north, Cornelia and Richard Clarke, had seen the fire engines that Sunday morning and telephoned Eszter to ask if we needed help. Learning that she would be alone for a few days, Cornelia insisted that Eszter come for dinner.

To take my mind off the itching corset and the itching empty space between my index and middle finger, Eszter gave a full account of her visit, from furnishings to food. All her enthusiasm was reserved for the baby chickens which the Clarkes's son had raised from fertile eggs as a high school biology project.

"You've just got to see them. They're so cute. They still look like eggs with feathers pasted on. Want to raise a few?"

Forgetting about my ribs, I bellowed, "NO!" When the pain had subsided, I added, "As it is, we're prisoners of the dogs and cats. You know I don't mind that, but caring for a bunch of stupid chickens will put us in solitary confinement. And I've heard they really are dumb."

"Who said anything about talking to them? All I'm interested in is fresh eggs every morning for breakfast. Doesn't that sound good?"

That was hitting below the belt. Eszter knew my specific fondness for eggs and my present preoccupation with anything I could put in my mouth which did not require inhaling. I went to sleep that night contemplating the taste of three poached eggs, well sprinkled with chives and cracked pepper, nesting on buttered sourdough toast. I woke up tasting them. Very good. A touch more salt, perhaps.

"Why are you smacking your lips like that?"

"Can't breathe very well with this thing on. My lips dry out. Listen, I was thinking maybe you're right. We should try a few hens. The place is fenced; there are plenty of greens around. All we'll have to do is throw them a little corn every day. If it doesn't work, if they're too much trouble, what have we lost? You make great chicken soup."

"Wonderful. I'll borrow Cornelia's incubator."

"Now, that's what I mean. Why make work for ourselves? We'll have to play nursemaid for six or eight months before they start to lay. As soon as I'm out of this straitjacket, I'll drive around and find six hens who are ready to go right to work."

Twenty to thirty years ago, the San Fernando Valley was a green checkerboard of orchards, ranches, and farms. Today it is a crazy quilt of urban sprawl. Cheap motels, "singles only" apartment complexes, plastic-flag-waving gas stations, and bottomless bars are slowly but surely squeezing the pleasure and pride out of having your own place. Valley residents are about to join America's new forgotten minority, the private homeowner. After hours of driving, I found only two old men who still sold poultry. One was going out of business: "I can't pay the taxes." The other seemed very disappointed that I did not want to buy his entire flock of a thousand white Leghorns: "I get the same price for eggs I got ten years ago, but the cost of feed has tripled. Are you sure you only want six?"

As she peeked into the burlap bag I had brought them home in, Eszter's reaction to my choice of hens was short of enthusiastic. "Why did you get all white ones? They come in a lot of other colors that would look much better." Before I could reply that I had not been out shopping for a car, Tiffany and Iago showed up. They clearly did not share Eszter's aesthetic reservations. The first chicken out of the sack and the place became a greyhound track. It was the feature race. The bell had sounded and the dogs were off and running. Iago was the favorite because he could see, but the smell of feathers and the sound of squawks was all that Tiffany needed. He was running only a half-length behind his father as the poor hen made it around the house for the first time. The gap widened on the second trip and on the third, Iago was the only pursuer. Tiffany had chosen to stand at the finish line with open mouth. He won.

Our vision of turning the place into a Currier & Ives barn-yard, with chickens free to scratch and roost at large, was not going to work. With the five hens locked up in the garage, I turned the car around and drove back to buy several rolls of wire fencing. This purchase was the first of chicken sundries which, over the next eight months, would finally average out at $.63 an egg or $1.89 per three-poached-egg breakfast. I am not including lawyer's fees. Neither was the cost of their house amortized. That was purchased years before.

When our two-car garage would no longer hold our one car because of the roadblocks of gardening equipment and stacks of fertilizer, I hunted about for a prefab toolshed. All the models available looked like portable aluminum rest rooms. We were going to build our own when Sears had a Holiday Season Special on A-frame playhouses, six by eight feet in size. The men who came to assemble it were concerned that our children would see it before Christmas morning. Too embarrassed to explain that they were going to all this trouble on Christmas Eve for a bunch of rakes, shovels, and steer manure and not wanting to spoil their pleasure in playing Santa Claus, I explained that the kids had colds and their mother was keeping them in bed until the next morning. Just as I finished the lie, Eszter arrived to see how things were going. The head Santa Claus asked her, "How are the little ones?" Thinking he was being facetious about Iago and Tiffany, who had kept the men in their truck when they arrived, she reassured him: "Fine, I just locked them up in the doghouse."

Getting back to the chickens—and I had to in a hurry because the garage was looking more and more like Jackson Pollock's studio—it was this playhouse which they inherited once the tools and machinery had been placed in the guest house storage room. It seemed pointless to move the bins of fertilizer. I nailed four laying boxes to the wall so that the birds would not have to waste their time standing in line for a nest. A "Push" sign, from an old swinging door, was hung above the boxes for all to see.

The morning after the birds took up residence, I made the toast and coffee while Eszter went out to collect the eggs. I insisted she carry a basket. I hoped only for three or four, but it would show the hens what was expected of them. No eggs. As a matter of fact, the next five breakfasts were also cholesterol-free. My explanation seemed logical: "New home and everything. I'm sure it takes time to adjust."

Fighting stoicism with hedonism, Eszter made an observation which would seem to bar her forever from any involvement in the Women's Liberation movement. "I don't blame them. What's the fun of having eggs or children if a man's not there at the beginning and the end? What those chickens need is a nice virile rooster. Then they'll perform." She followed with a well-rehearsed afterthought:

"You know, Cornelia says their roosters are fighting all the time and we'd be doing her a favor if we took the loser. His name is Rusty, but we can change that." We never did, probably because the gold-and-orange-feathered fellow belied his name.

The morning after Rusty was formally introduced to the

Leghorns, Eszter's basket held five blushing eggs. "See, they wanted to show their appreciation." In defense of credulity and man's right to grow bored, such 100 per cent production never occurred again. But Eszter and Rusty started a courtship which, as far as she was concerned, made up for an occasionally empty egg cup. Every morning he waited impatiently for his champion to open the gate to the chicken run. As soon as Eszter stepped inside, Rusty ruffled his feathers and performed a sort of Indian ceremonial dance around her feet. He stopped this circular shagging only when he got his wish: to be picked up and petted. If Eszter stroked his emerging comb sufficiently and tickled his wattles, Rusty regarded her with a sample of his new-found voice. It was a perfect falsetto crow.

Once Rusty discovered he could half-climb, half-fly over the fence, he gave up waiting for Eszter to come say good morning. When she opened the French doors in the bedroom, there he was strutting about on the brick steps, pausing now and then to blow himself up to crowing pitch. In the beginning the sound he made was so feeble, the doors had to be wide open for us to hear the off-key greeting. Of course, the appearance of Iago and Tiffany would break up these courting sessions. At the sound of their approach, he hurried back to his five wives.

For the first six weeks or so, the Danes were fascinated by these smelly white things. They would sit for hours, noses mashed against the fencing, watching the hens move from scratch to worm and back to scratch. Tiffany sensed they were near, but only knew of their immediacy when his nose was pecked. He liked this blindman's buff and would bark for more. Iago, on the other hand, being the brains of the family, soon tired of a game which smacked too much of Pavlovian cheating. He moved off to fairer sport, like squirrels and rabbits. The latter, though, were quick in spreading the word on how to outsmart the big black brute. Whenever Iago managed to corner a hare, to find himself nose to nose with a succulent dinner, as soon as he opened his salivating mouth the rabbit would run straight between his front paws and under the arch of his rear legs. Iago followed the escaping animal with his head, thereby doing a somersault and ending up on his back, empty stomach aloft.

Pancake and Petunia, on the other hand, showing greater foresight than their owners, would have stopped this whole chicken foolishness had it not been for Rusty. For the first few days the Siamese were content to stand around, two housewives at the butcher's discussing which was the plumpest hen. It would have been easier for them to make their selection had they been able to poke and pinch the merchandise, but my fence stood in the way. Anyone who has attempted to stretch chicken wire across a sloping terrain knows the frustrations of trying to keep taut the flimsy fencing. One of my mottoes has always been "Avoid frustration whenever possible." According to Eszter, I have lived up to the slogan, but it is accurate only with the substitution of "work" for "frustration." In this case, she was willing to admit that my halfway measures had a certain merit. The fence was so wobbly, Pancake and Petunia were unable to scale it. Tired of repeatedly falling off the shaky, paw-cutting barrier, they decided to pick up their poultry order by subterfuge.

The tunnel they constructed, one wide enough for a pound-and-a-half broiler and a fourteen-pound Siamese, was nearly completed when Rusty arrived from the Clarkes'. With all the new admiring ladies about, the rooster forgot his recent defeats and strutted about with sultanly sway. Unaware of the new tenant, Pancake was busy breaking through the last inch of sod. So as not to litter his tunnel, he was now working backward, kicking the last chunks of pawed-out earth into the chicken area, confident that behind his back cowered a week of extracurricular eating. Heady with the exaltation of finally being master and sole protector, Rusty pounced upon Pancake's back and began taking peck-size samples of the cat's scalp. Hisses and hair filled the air. Pancake's retreat was so auditory that Petunia, mid-tunnel, saw no reason to wait for an explanation. Seconds later, she was sitting in their favorite hiding place, under our bed, commiserating with Pancake and licking his wounds. From then on, the two cats boycotted that particular poultry shop. Only pressing business—a surfacing gopher or a fresh bird's nest—would tempt them to go anywhere near the hen house. And on those rare occasions, they slunk past the enclosure, eyes averted, voices muted.

Kati was a distant observer to this aborted foraging expedition. She was a hunt-and-tease cat, not a hunt-and-eater. Her idea of blood sports was to escort a tiny lizard or field mouse to the confines of the kitchen, where she could play swat and run. When her prey ran one way, Kati scooted the other, wide-eyed in surprise that her tentative paw swipe could trigger such an exciting response. If one of her pounces drew blood by mistake, Kati retreated in shame and the wounded playmate was free to make his or her way out the cat door to freedom. It was her flirtations with danger, this yes-no fascination with the exciting movements and noises of life, which led to Kati's accidental death.

We had let the guest house stand empty as long as our conscience and bank balance would permit and then placed another ad. This time "single person only" was in boldface capitals. And contrary to all we stood for, we had no intention of being Equal Opportunity landlords. When it came to the sex of the tenant, only males had a chance. Our final choice was very much that.

In Andrew Smith, a handsome New York writer come West for the gold, we finally found the ingredients which made for a painless tenant. Andrew's talents were in great demand. He worked at CBS from ten in the morning to eight at night fashioning ad-lib remarks to be bounced about on the network's late-night talk show. And his company was in such demand by so many different women, he never wanted any of them to know where he lived. Since one can hardly say to a young lady, "Let's go back to my place for a nightcap," and then blindfold her, he never had company. The only sign that Andrew was in residence was an occasional overflowing cesspool. He showered and shaved a lot.

Gentlemanly and civilized, Andrew had gone Hollywood in but one respect. He leased an XKE and drove it much too fast. There is something about our driveway which brings out the cowboy in sports car drivers. The thirty-five-degree upward pitch of the blacktop must induce Walter Mitty fantasies of Grand Prix duels through the Alps. Kati, with her fascination for the unusual, was the only one who enjoyed listening to Andrew rev up his motor and mash gears as he set off for his appointed rounds. She watched his comings and goings from a grandstand seat atop a stump near the drive. With all that horsepower charging about, we began locking up the dogs each night for safety sake. Last thing before going to bed, I would take them out for a final walk. It was on one of these nightly strolls that I saw Kati killed.

Iago and Tiffany had finished their recycling among the white marguerites in the lower field—with just the stars for light, the daisy bushes become a village of snow-frosted igloos—and the three of us were on the way back to the house. We passed Kati hiding among the ferns which circled her lookout stump and I told her to come on home; but like most loners, she took invitations as a challenge and stayed right where she was. A second or two later, the sound of Andrew's car coming up the hill filled the night and I called the dogs out of the way. As I held them by their collars, waiting for the Jaguar to slow down, out of the corner of my eye I saw Kati dash across the drive in front of the car.

When one's ears are not perfect, the eyes have a way of hearing; so while I could never swear to the fact, I was sure I had heard the bumper thud at the very moment when it seemed the gray ball was going to make the other side of the road.

Andrew said he neither heard nor felt anything. I am sure

he did not. Kati was such a cushion of furry softness the sound of her impact would have been drowned out to the person sitting behind that zooming engine. For over an hour, the two of us called and hunted for Kati by flashlight. Iago knew what we were after and he joined in, sniffing through the ivy and brush which bordered the gully side of the drive. Nothing. Eszter was asleep. There was no point in telling her until morning. There was the feeble hope that the cat had merely fled in fright and would return home later, unhurt. She did not, of course, and at daylight the search continued.

From before breakfast to after lunch—she forgot both meals—Eszter crisscrossed the entire property calling and crying for Kati. Almost worse than the fear of stumbling upon her dead body was the thought that the little cat was lying injured someplace, needing our help, and we could not find her to give it. Andrew and I quietly gave up an hour or so before Eszter returned to the house. It was the first time I had ever seen anyone physically exhausted from crying. She had lost her voice, so it was in a hoarse whisper that Eszter forced herself to say it, "Kati's dead. I would have heard her crying or she would have come when I called. She was so small." Nevertheless, I know that for months, each time Eszter reached into her basket of embroidery yarn she expected to find a blue-gray ball. It had always been Kati's favorite napping spot. The urge and need were there to take out on Andrew our anger and sorrow, but he was crying too.

Now that we had established a fenced-in area, far from the swimming pool, I was not at all surprised when Eszter came home with three Muscovy ducks—girl, boy, and a back-up girl. Eszter could not very well excuse the newcomers by saying that the chickens needed company, so we got right down to her true motive. "Wait till you see how cute ducklings are. They'll follow us all over the place." Being shadowed by a troop of ducklings was precisely what I did not want.

Having Iago and Tiffany in my wake was quite enough adulation for one man. But our problem was bigger than that. I wanted to taste the eggs Eszter had been talking about for so long, she wanted to hatch them. "Don't worry. I'm sure both ducks won't set at the same time. You can have the eggs from under the one that's standing." It must be admitted, the two ducks were very cooperative—so was the drake. They followed our game plan precisely. While one gave motherly concentration to hatching, the other, a true trollop, spent her days making love with Gunár, taking time away from these brazen exhibitions only to drop and hide an egg in her basket each morning. After my first sampling of these very special, lusty-tasting gifts, it was obvious why the duck went to such pains to hide her treasure from the greedy eyes of man under layers and layers of straw. Chickens, on the other hand, aware that their product is bland and common in comparison, leave their eggs lying about for anyone to pick up and eat, including their cannibalistic relatives.

Also, unlike the five Leghorns, the Muscovites had personality and deserved the dignity of names. "*Gunár*" is Hungarian for "gander," but by the time Eszter realized her mistake it was too late to change. Besides, I could not pronounce "*kacsa*." The drake's two wives were called "Rubber" and "Satchmo." Ever since I had the questionable distinction of being a hearing-aid-wearing jazz critic for *Esquire*, Louis Armstrong was on my list of musical geniuses. It was nice to have a pet who could aptly carry his nickname, especially when the sobriquet recalled an anecdote of Armstrong humor.

Years ago I made my regular twenty-four-month visit to the dentist. Supposedly adjusted friends—they are always the ones who "adore" bullfights—tell me they leave the dental chair saying, "Thank you, Doctor, see you again in six months." I escape from the stocks perspiring and faint and simply ask if I may use his sink to wash up. On this particular occasion, as I sponged away the telltale signs of cowardice, the dentist's wristwatch caught my twitching eye. It was hanging from a hook on the wall, back forward. Below the twenty-four-carat mark was this inscription:

Dear Manny,
Thanks for the choppers
They're the greatest
Love, Satchmo.

Each morning the ducks waddled over to greet me at the gate, much in the manner of Rusty, though they danced to a different tune, that of the Big Bands in the late thirties. They "Pecked," the graceful body step which punctuated The Big Apple. The choreography called for a stiff upper body and undulating movement of head and neck, resulting in alternate visits to your partner's left and right ear lobe. Gunár, Rubber, and Satchmo did the step with Rockette precision. There was talking in the chorus line which I could not hear. *Déjà vu.* Spike had returned to haunt me. Eszter gave quick assurance: One, Muscovites are practically voiceless; they are advertised as "the quackless duck"; two, I wasn't missing anything, since the ducks were simply asking "How do you do?" over and over again.

Now that I knew what they were saying and that the words coincided with the rhythmic pecking, Eszter and I found ourselves emulating their neck movement and saying "How do you do?" in turn. What goes on between man and pet should, of course, be in sanctum sanctorum. But since we allowed our very best friends to witness this ritual of bowing and scraping, this after-you-Alphonse charade, it is only fair to quote Cynthia Lindsay as she got down on her knees and joined us in the salutation, "You two are crazy."

Their initial politeness was all sham. Within weeks, the three ducks were engaged in the most treacherous form of backbiting. And it was mine, not Eszter's back, that they were chewing up. I found it impossible to fill the feed trough or change their straw without receiving a nip on the calf or a flying gouge in the small of the back. Noting my obvious displeasure at these attacks, Rusty immediately joined in the sport. Henceforth, except when guests were about praising our devoted husbandry and admiring the gizzard-shaped concrete pool I had poured for the ungrateful ducks, I never entered the poultry area unarmed. A broken bamboo rake proved most effective. It cut a wide swath and made a resounding noise on impact.

Although the rooster and ducks united in making my life miserable, once I had backed out the gate, they started to fight among themselves. Clearly, chickens and ducks are not birds of a feather. Given time, they might have eliminated each other, but Eszter would have no part of my murderous plan and insisted that some sort of DMZ be established between the warring factions. People have a terrible habit of asking what we do on weekends. In those days, I was quick to answer "Nothing." While not a very informative reply, somehow it seemed a great deal more entertaining than, "Dug some more fence holes and built a separate house for the ducks," "The chickens got mites. Had to powder them and wash down their house with disinfectant," or "Satchmo was about to hatch, so we canceled all dates and sat up with her."

We were especially curious about Satchmo's progeny because, when she and Rusty were not fighting, they were making violent love. Actually, the sound and fury emanated from Rusty, who just could not get it through his libido that all girls are not chickens. Satchmo, while flattered by the advances, knew the sad difference between a drake and a rooster and patiently squatted in the grass until the mixed-up kid was exhausted. Her acquiescence was doubly selfless, for during the trysts Rusty gradually denuded the nape of her neck. On one occasion—the first and last—his pecking drew blood. Satchmo retaliated by piggybacking the rooster over to the duck pond and jumping in. Gunár was very "now" about this one-sided affair and turned his head the other way. The drake was far wiser than Eszter and I, for we thought that Rusty's efforts might just possibly bear fruit in the arrival of some crossbreeds, which we had decided to call "Dickens."

Satchmo's six 100 per cent Muscovy ducklings, innocent as

they were, are what really put us on the expressway to folly. Cornelia fell in love with the babies and begged Eszter for two of them. In return she would give us a pair of Rhode Island Reds. From then on, the two women were swapping chickens like youngsters at a stamp club. When they ran out of breeds to exchange, they bought new strains, each trying to top the other with the exoticism of their purchase. By the time the neighborhood swap meet was over, our hen house had become a UN of the chicken world. There were Long-tailed Yokohamas, Mottled Javas, Danish Brown Leghorns, Cornish Bantams, Russian Orloffs, and heading the Committee on Civil Rights, White-faced Black Spanish.

With this international assortment of hens for companion-ship, it was no great surprise when Rusty skipped adolescence and found his adult voice. But the power and penetrating pitch of the crow was startling. While very proud of the sound, even he could not get over it and each of his cock-a-doodle-doos ended with a question mark. Reveille came about 5:00 A.M., give or take fifteen minutes of sleep. The first time Eszter was awakened by the sound, she wanted to go out in the dark and dew to congratulate Rusty on his coming of age. The next morning she woke me up to ask how I could sleep through the crowing and then buried her head in two pillows, hers and mine. The third day there was no problem. Eszter was back on earplugs.

Being in bed with a woman whose ears are stopped with wax corks is like lying in your analyst's office. From neither can you enlist a response. To lessen my feelings of exile, I repeated news of a medical breakthrough, overheard at the feed store: With a minor operation, roosters could have their vocal cords silenced.

"Not on your life. Never. Do you want to emasculate Rusty?"

I had picked up another bit of chicken lore while waiting at the granary for the car's springs to be sprung with sacks of laying mash, scratch, duck pellets, drums of insecticide, and bales of straw. I mentioned to the fellow with the baling hooks that our hens had started following Rusty over the fence, and the garden was starting to look like an Apollo close-up of the moon.

"Nuttin' to it, bud. Just take a pair of dem scissors and cut dem wings. Don't hurt dem a damn bit."

While I held, Eszter did the tonsorial trimming with the same pinking shears we had used on Iago's umbilical cord. The final effect was quite fetching, reminiscent of Sophia Loren and Anna Magnani in those films where they had been mistaken for collaborators and their hair was just starting to grow back. But what the docking boss had failed to mention was that you are only supposed to cut the wing feathers on one side thereby creating an aerodynamic imbalance. Our hens could still fly the coop if they had a good updraft and flapped extra hard.

Cornelia's rooster began trying to top Rusty's every crow. With the guest house halfway between both chicken ranches, poor Andrew was left as the best judge of which had the better voice. He never complained. On the contrary, there was charming small talk about how he liked the country sounds and pastoral memories of his birthplace back in Connecticut and that he slept like a log when he was not taking showers. "Besides, I'm working on a screenplay of my own and if Rusty doesn't get me up at five, it'll never be finished." Andrew's lovely lies were his memorial to Kati; but Eszter and I knew that sooner or later something had to be done about those noisy, messy, time-consuming, garden-wrecking fowl. For the moment we settled for later.

12

The Only Answer to Death

Instead of being a superstitious person, I have a pressing conscience. Perhaps they are one and the same. The latter continually nudges me with the dark thought that evil begets evil. When a personal misfortune occurs, I run through my mental Rolldex of deeds which should not have been done, thoughts that were wrong to think, trying to find the reason why.

When Iago had to be put to death, I went back and forth through these well-thumbed cards of guilt. On none was scribbled a wrong equal to the loss, for I loved that beautiful black Dane more than any other animal. More than any other person, after Eszter, my daughter, Beatrice, and a few very special people. While all the animals have always been "ours," receiving equal love and attention, Eszter and I have always known that Dorka was emotionally her dog, Iago mine. Dorka came when Eszter was alone, Iago to a man who had never had a dog before. But whomever he had belonged to, Iago would have been himself—manly, beautiful, and gently kind.

Had some armchair psychiatrist at a stand-up cocktail party told me I took Iago's death so badly because it reminded me of my father's end, I would have excused myself, saying my hearing-aid battery was dead, and gone to get another drink. But the roving fraud might have sensed a certain truth. Both had strength, dignity, and kindness. They had style. Enjoying every minute of their lives, those they were near could not help but do the same. Both died of cancer long before they should have. My father, who loved animals, would not have minded this comparison.

I was taking Tiffany to the vet for a shot. Southern California's dry climate causes all sorts of skin rashes in Danes. Tiffany has had them all and a few extra which are still being researched. Iago went along for the ride. He liked nothing quite so much as regally sitting in the back of the open car, nose to the wind, eyes scanning the populace for a barkable subject.

Tiffany was Dr. Sprowl's last patient, so after stuffing my pockets with an array of anti-scratch pills and a bottle of dermicide shampoo, we walked together to the parking lot. Iago swiveled his head in our direction.

"When did he get that bump on his head?"

I noticed a very slight swelling on his black velvet forehead, directly over the right eye. "You've got better eyes than I have, Doctor. What is it? A bruise?"

Sprowl softly pressed his fingers on either side of the swollen spot. Iago pulled back his head in pain. "It may be. I don't have to ask how he's eating. He never looked in better shape. But just in case, bring him back inside for an X ray."

I asked, "What's 'in case'?"

"A tumor."

The plates showed a growth of some sort and Sprowl suggested I leave the dog overnight. He would do a biopsy first thing in the morning. Waiting for the results, Estzer and I told each other that nothing could be seriously wrong. And we both believed it. Iago seemed to have finally adjusted to Dorka's absence. He was his bouncy, vital self, once again very interested in measuring the hemline of women's skirts. The tests were positive. He had fibrosarcoma.

Sprowl is a shy man, one of few words. On this occasion he made what amounted to a speech, "I'm afraid the tumor is in a spot where we can't operate, Mr. Colen. I'm sorry to have to recommend it twice in less than a year; nevertheless, if Iago were my dog, I would put him to sleep. Right now, while he's still a very happy, beautiful animal. It is not going to hurt him, but trying to keep the dog alive will destroy the two of you. I know, I've seen it happen. Veterinarians have one very humane advantage over regular doctors; when a case is hopeless, we can prescribe euthanasia and save everyone great pain." During all of this, Sprowl had been holding and petting Iago. Now he released him and the dog bounded over to us. He started nudging first Eszter, then me, wanting to get out of the clinic and back home. It all came down to just that: I could not say: "No, Iago, you cannot ever again go home with us."

"Doctor, there must be something we can do?" The words were a question, my inflection a plea.

"One of the best radiologists in the country is in Pasadena. Using cobalt treatments, he might be able to arrest the growth. The quicker he sees Iago the better. These things spread very fast." The last was a compassionate understatement.

That afternoon we drove Iago to Pasadena. He seemed to like this much maligned community, not because of the wonderful old houses creaking to the mansards with Republicans, but because it took so long to get there. He had plenty of time to pose in the back seat for passing motorists. The squeal of brakes as the admiring drivers returned their eyes to the road was music to his ears.

Dr. Thom was Jean Hersholt without the pipe. Knowing that dogs do not insist on antiseptic white jackets, he dressed as a friend. Iago sniffed his tweeds and they were instant buddies. Now that the dog was at ease, the doctor turned to reassure us. "Please don't worry, he doesn't feel a thing. I'm going to take some new X rays and then give him his first treatment. Take about two hours. Why don't you folks do a little sightseeing."

Touring Pasadena is hardly the most diverting way to spend an afternoon. The effort of putting on the annual Rose Parade seems to drain the town of all life and warmth for the next 364 days. We went and had too many cups of coffee and then visited a friend who ran an antique shop. After I dropped and paid for a mercury glass candlestick, we went back to Thom's. As we entered, the doctor was just leading Iago out of the radiology room. As a carry-over from the deaf years, I still concentrate my attention on people's lips. There was a slight sag in the corners of Thom's mouth as he spoke.

"Hard to believe there's anything wrong with that dog. Look how fast he snapped out of the anesthesia." Iago was prancing about the reception room, licking the secretary's knees, doing the same to Thom's shoes, and finishing off with a thorough wash of Eszter's face. "But there is, Mr. Colen, and I can't do anything about it."

With his specialized equipment he had taken a more complete set of X rays. One by one he held them up to the light. "You see, the cancer has metastasized from the tissue growth Dr. Sprowl found to this whole bone area of the skull. I might have been able to stop the first, but the second growth is smack in the center of everything vital. I could say, 'Sure, come back next week for another treatment, but it would be a waste of money. Much more important, and what I care about, it would be a cruel waste of your hope."

I remember very little about the trip home except that Eszter sat in the back seat with her arm around Iago's shoulders and that when we got out of the car I asked her what she had been thinking on the silent journey. "About you and Dorka and the tiny pool house and how you ran up the hill with newborn Iago yelling for scissors to cut the cord."

There was a message with the answering service to call Dr. Sprowl when we got in. Eszter stands beside me while I dial, holding my free hand. Her lower lip is bitten white from holding back the tears, a chalk mark on a flush-red face. "I just called, Mr. Colen, to say that Dr. Thom spoke to me after you left. I know how you two feel. I've gotten to hate the word 'sorry,' but I don't know what else to use. Have you made up your mind yet?"

I am trying to think clearly; yet I hear myself using the worst of soap opera clichés: "How long does he have to live, Doctor?" A preposterous question, one which only a fool would ask and a knave dare answer. Sprowl is certainly not that.

"It's impossible to tell. Weeks, months—maybe six. Toward the end it gets very painful and messy for the dog, and for you."

"Is he in pain now?"

"Not yet. Uncomfortable is a better word. As though you had a bad head cold. You'll know when it hurts."

I looked up at Eszter absently shaking her head back and forth, as though she could hear the other side of the conversation and read my thoughts, too. "I can't do it, Doctor. He's too full of life. Everything happened so quickly."

"Maybe that's where you're lucky, Mr. Colen. Don't wait too long."

"Long" was a short, terrible three weeks. There was no lessening of Iago's high spirits, but each day he left more in his feeding bowl. When Tiffany tried to lick clean the biopsy scar, there were ominous growls. Sensing something was wrong, the son started eating less. Since Iago, like his mother, was now happiest curled up to Eszter on the embroidery couch, we decided to go further and let him sleep in our room at night. As the final step, so that Iago would have his whole family around him, a sleeping pad was rolled out for Tiffany too. But in the last week Iago started to have nosebleeds and the smell of the blood frightened Tiffany. (I wanted to call Sprowl and find out what to do about the bleeding, but I knew what he would say.) He barked and whined constantly. We put him back in the doghouse.

Even then, neither of us got much sleep. We lay awake listening to Iago's increasingly heavy breathing, knowing that the morning would bring the inevitable one day nearer. During the daytime hours, each was aware that the other was secretly looking, wondering who would have the courage to say what had to be said. Constantly on edge, guarding against talking of the happy past or about the sad future, we started fighting over idiotic things: Did I remember to give Iago his vitamin pills? Should he be covered with a blanket at night? How many aspirin is enough to kill whatever pain he might have?

And then, at the end of the third week, a private remembrance brought us back to reality. Iago was having a particularly bad night breathing. I got out of bed, collected Q-Tips and baby oil from the bathroom, and sat down with his shiny black head in my lap. Halfway through the slow process of swabbing out his nostrils, Iago pulled his head aside, licked my nose, and then just stared at me. Looking back at his big brown eyes, I suddenly thought of Beth, who had gone alone to Switzerland so that she might die in peace, and dignity, free of guilty mourners standing in the wings. Eszter was watching me as I whispered, "I'll call Sprowl in the morning."

Just before dawn, I had seen Eszter quietly slide out of bed and slip down beside Iago to kiss and whisper her goodbyes. When I led him out of the room an hour later, she pretended sleep, although the covers around her curled body trembled. It was not masochism which made me see to it that this morning was as normal as every other, for my real urge was to get it over with as soon as possible. But to rush Iago's last few hours, to give him short shrift now, because it eased my pain, would have been a shabby denial of the love and respect we had professed these past ten-plus years.

I took Iago and Tiffany down to the gate for the paper and watched them run back up the hill, white wigwag flags flapping from their jaws. Now the older, Iago was entrusted with the sections we cared about reading. It was Tiffany's turn to salivate over real estate and used cars. I prepared their usual full-size breakfast, although certain that Iago, at least, would take only a bite or two. I left them standing by their feed stands and went inside to call Dr. Sprowl. "I'm bringing Iago over." There was a long pause; then: "I'll leave word to get me out of surgery when you come." Putting down the phone, I noticed a Librium capsule Eszter had put there for me sometime during the night. When I went to get Iago, his bowl had been licked clean, the first time in three weeks. Hearing the clink of the car keys, Tiffany was insistent that he go, too. I locked him in the doghouse.

The drive was almost the worst part, the beginning of the breakdown I had known was coming from the moment I opened my eyes and realized what day it was. When Dorka had made the same journey she was a tired old lady, too exhausted to lift her head above the dashboard. But Iago—Iago sat on his haunches beside me in the front seat, head held high, eyes and ears at attention taking in the sights and sounds of a fresh new day. He looked so alive, so happy, it was very hard to believe that this was a merciful trip and not simply the preamble to a senseless, calculated killing. By the time we arrived at the clinic my mouth was dry from having repeated over and over again the four words he liked to hear most: Iago's a beautiful dog.

Doris, the head of the office, led us to a room opposite the surgery. We avoided each other's eyes and she quietly shut the door upon leaving. When Sprowl came in—he had knocked first—I was kneeling on the floor with my arms around Iago saying, "I'm sorry."

"There's nothing else you could have done, Mr. Colen."

Suddenly, I needed somebody to blame, someone I could see to vent my anger and sadness upon. Sprowl was it. I hated him. But just as quickly, before striking out with words, my body started to quake in dry sobs and heaves. And then the tears came. A worried Iago jumped up on me, putting his paws on my shoulders. I tried to stop, but the effort triggered more. Sprowl turned his back and pretended to be straightening out a tray of instruments. When the room was quiet again, he turned around and looked down at the dog.

"Please take him, Doctor."

He started to hand me Iago's collar and leash. I shook my head and started to cry again. At the door, with his hand on Iago's head, Sprowl turned to say, "If you want to stay here for a while, you can. No one will disturb you."

Driving home, I decided it was a very special man you could cry in front of and feel no shame.

The United Parcel truck was halfway down the drive, when Eszter caught me with the package from the crematorium.

"I never asked before because I didn't know what to do with them. Where did you put Dorka's ashes?" They were hidden in a place she would never search, at the bottom of a box of canceled checks in the storeroom. "Now I know where we should put Dorka and Iago. Come see."

Eszter led me to the doghouse area. She had already weeded and cultivated the basin under the Babcock peach. It was the right choice. I spaded both boxes of ashes into the soil, then Eszter planted two packages of forget-me-nots and watered them in. Lost, bewildered Tiffany paced between us. He had no idea of what was going on, but it had to be something special. Why else would they be clinking glasses when it was nowhere near cocktail time?

Tiffany was right about the hour. The sun was high in the sky when we decided to have a picnic in the shade of this lovely tree. The sound he heard was our wine glasses touching as we toasted memories and talked of the future. Looking toward the doghouse, I watched Tiffany lapping water from the one remaining feeding stand. The other two had been stored away.

"I just remembered how I used to say, 'Excuse me' or, 'I'm sorry' if I bumped into the dogs while they were eating.

When you catch yourself doing it, talking to them like humans, you feel so silly."

Eszter smiled. "Or, 'I beg your pardon.'"

"It seems so empty around here. How do we fill the void?"

Eszter answered, "With life."

There was no question about it, the three of us needed those three feeding stands back in full operation. The two of us agreed—I was now a dues-paying loyal member of the There's Nothing Like a Dane Club—that the most fun would be to start all over with a harlequin bitch and let her take it from there. But for the time being, we would have to forgo such plans. After years of being either totally ignored or called "those spotted dogs, sorta like Dalmatians," harlequin Danes were "in" and their price was going way out of bounds. Breeders asked five to six hundred dollars for a well-marked, well-bred female. I had just sat down to write this book and Eszter was back looking at the television program for old movies to embroider by, since she had been commissioned to design a line of needlework kits for the country's largest manufacturer. Sales and royalties for both were eighteen months away. We had to watch our money very carefully, especially with Mr. Nixon's economic game plan going for us. Our hopes of getting back into the Dane business would have to wait until seventy-two, when we found out if the American public liked our efforts—and Mr. Nixon's.

The nation was trading down to smaller cars; it was time we tried a compact dog. It would do Tiffany no harm to learn that the words "dog" and "Dane" were not one and the same.

Eszter turned chauvinistic. She wanted a puli, like the ones her grandfather had raised in Hungary. "They're very smart. He used them for herding sheep. If we got one there'd be no damn chickens in my garden. And they look so funny with all that hair drooling down their face."

Number one, I like to see animals' and people's eyes. A dog hiding behind nose-level bangs has the same disquieting effect upon me as a person who lives in sunglasses. I want to say to both, "Come on out where I can see you." Secondly, since our animals shared every room in the house with the exception of the bath—Correction: both the cats and dogs were in the habit of drinking fresh water from the toilet bowl—I was against a long-haired permanent house guest. As it was, during the Embroidery Season, an independent survey of each week's vaccum cleaner bag showed seven parts of wool, floss, mohair, and angora snips to three parts dog and cat hairs. It was hard to be too critical of the former falling in Eszter's wake, for the litter had a beautiful way of returning to nature. Each spring, the birds beat the garbageman to the trash barrels and made their nests from the scraps of multicolored yarn. Their homes in hanging baskets, tucked under eaves and balanced on branches, looked like gay miniature Easter baskets.

Having blackballed pulis, it was now my turn to vote. "How about a boxer or a Doberman?"

"I've still got a thing about anything German, even their dogs."

"Danes are German."

"That's entirely different. They don't look it."

The debate dragged on, neither showing total enthusiasm for the other's canine selection. Then one Sunday we read an article about the new breeding and training facilities in Los Angeles for Seeing Eye dogs. The paragraph which interested us most explained that only the better-natured female German shepherds were trained to work with the blind. The males were for sale.

Ever since having had to leave Eszter for three months in 1964, while working in Paris, we often talked about having a trained watchdog around the place. The daylight pleasures of seclusion have an insidious way of inviting fear when there is only one to turn on the lights. Dorka's sheer size might frighten an intruder, but her bites could not be counted on. As for Iago, it would not have surprised me to come home one evening and find him holding the flashlight for a burglar. In the same situation, Tiffany would have gone to look for fresh batteries. During our 1964 separation, I hired a private patrol service to check out the place each evening. Eszter called me in Paris to complain about the privacy part of the arrangement.

"Hello? I can't hear you. I miss you something awful. Who's there with you?"

"Where are you? It's five in the morning here."

"Well, it's ten P.M. L.A. time and there's a man creeping around outside shooting a flashlight in the bedroom window."

"What are you doing?"

"Lying on the floor where he can't see me. You hired a Peeping Tom to look after me."

"Where are the dogs?"

"On the bed. They barked once and went back to sleep."

"The patrol guy just wants to see who's there and that you're okay."

"Then why does he never flash that searchlight in my face? It's always focused on my bosom."

I imagine that evening was in Eszter's mind when she took the Eye Dog Foundation article over to the telephone. In less than five minutes she had traced down the man in charge of the kennel, ordered a puppy, and was back reporting the other end of the conversation. "They don't expect another litter for five weeks and then we'll have to wait another six until we can bring him home, but the man promised he'd save the best one for us. They're all champion stock and he'll show us how to train ours into a real guard dog."

"You know what you just did, don't you? You bought a long-haired German dog."

"Well, we'll call him an Alsatian, like they do in Europe. And if you brush him every day, there won't be so many hairs around the house."

Three months was a long time to wait to fill the gap left by Iago's death, so for interim companionship two new kittens were adopted, What-a-Puss and Ping-Pong.

13

What-a-Puss and Ping-Pong

When Eszter is away from her home supply of pets, she had an unfailing knack for finding substitutes. I pick my airplane seat after calculating the distance to the nearest exit, Eszter sits down next to the woman whose carryall seems most likely to contain a smuggled pet. According to the commercials, everyone chooses his gasoline station after inspecting the rest rooms; we slow down only if there is a lost dog hanging around the lube rack. Once, at the San Ysidro Ranch in Montecito, we ended up with the one cottage whose fireplace housed a very tame chipmunk.

What-a-Puss "happened" in much the same way.

We were driving back along the Coast Highway after a business trip to San Francisco. The scenery is so spectacular around Big Sur that to speed by is truly un-American. The night was spent at the Highland Inn. The walls of the lodge's cocktail lounge are papered with the usual photos of celebrities who had slept there. But this collection contained a surprising number of cat photographs. One in particular, a magnificently huge white Persian, was upstaging Kim Novak, Rita Hayworth, Bob Hope, and Konrad Adenauer.

Eszter asked the bartender where she could find the owner of this beautiful cat (she slipped and said, "beautiful Kati"). He pointed toward heaven.

"That's too bad. Anybody who owned such a special animal must have been wonderful. Now, that's someone I would have liked to know."

"She is, ma'am, she owns this place." The bartender had been gesturing toward the owner's cottage nestled among huge redwoods on a bluff overlooking the bass-drum-pounding, rock-rimmed surf of Big Sur. He *had* been pointing out a spot very close to heaven.

Eszter turned to me, her face one big smile. "May I?" By the question I knew her to mean could she be excused to go visit the owner and if any descendants of the pinup Persian were for sale might she buy one? An hour later, I looked down at the bar and decided I had had either too much to drink or not enough. A fresh large bowl of potato chips had been pushed in my direction. The contents were moving.

"Go ahead, take one. They won't bite you." Eszter had returned. That was how, in collusion with management, she introduced me to our new friend. Pushing aside a few chips revealed a chinchilla-colored pelt about the size of my hand. The kitten was very high fashion—all eyes, penciled round with white mascara. Between the two yellow gemstones, black worry lines ran up the bridge of her nose and fanned out across a silver-gray brow. Eszter asked, "Have you ever seen such a puss?" We eventually discovered that What-a-Puss's concerned expression was a cover-up for the whims of a shameless vamp.

Trouble boiled in paradise when the three of us returned from Big Sur. The house sitter, a lovely girl who often helped Eszter with embroidery projects, met us at the front door with rage in her dark Italian eyes. "Eszter, you know how much I love the animals, but I'll never stay here alone again."

My first reaction was that Andrew had had the good sense
to make a pass at this beautiful, seductive girl; but it turned
out to be the ducks and the rooster who did the attacking.
Frances's arms had bill bruises, and Rusty had actually punc-
tured her leg with his spurs. "How can you live with those
horrible birds?" It was a good question. The answer was we
could not if we wished to keep our sanity, our tenant, and
future house sitter. The problem: how to do away with these
spoilers of domestic tranquility?

The man who had sold me the first six Leghorns smiled
sadly and shook his head as I proposed paying him five dollars
to take back the whole flock. "I'm gettin' out, too, mister."
Driving back from this no-sale, passing a Colonel Sanders
bucket in the sky, I realized why that white-haired gentleman was always smiling: he was in the business of killing
chickens, not raising them. If he could do it, why not I?
Eszter went along with my proposal on condition that Rusty
was pardoned and she did not have to see or hear the bloody
deed or know when it was going to take place. Secretly, my
wish was the same; but there was no backing down, for I had
been full of big talk about Man the Hunter and Provider and
how it was hypocritical to cringe at killing a chicken since
we were not vegetarians.

As a reluctant poultryman, one of the more useless bits of
information I had learned was that chickens are most easily
caught at sundown when they repair to their roost and fall
into a somnambulistic stupor. This merciful hour was chosen
to decimate their ranks. Armed with a large Japanese cleaver,
normally used for splitting dog bones, and a burlap bag, I entered the chicken house. Rusty greeted my arrival with an
apprehensive rustle of feathers. My well-thought-out plan
had three stages: drop slumbering hen into sack, hold hen's
head through burlap cover, drop Japanese guillotine on neck.
That way I would not witness the execution, my hands would
go unstained. Between roost and bottom of gunnysack, the
first hen woke up cackling and crashing about to such an
alarming degree that I was unable to accomplish Step Two.

When I returned to the house, Eszter asked what all the noise had been about. Following the terms of our agreement, I explained that a duck had strayed into the chicken section and started fighting.

The next time I tried to do what is supposed to come naturally to man, I had a bottle of chloroform and a wad of cotton in my pocket. Very proud of my ingenuity, I was now able to advance to Step Three. Unfortunately, even with the burlap cloth hiding the anesthetized chicken, my eyes turned away as the cleaver descended. The only blood that evening dripped from a nick on my finger, caused at the moment of truth. On the way to the Band-Aid box, I remembered those black-suited men of western films and decided to call upon the services of a traveling executioner.

Through the years we discovered that there were certain gardening tasks—transplanting trees, Rototilling, and the like —for which Eszter had neither the muscle nor the machinery. To help her out, a strong Dutchman, Peter, drops by for a few hours each week. It says "Gardener" on his monthly bill although Peter is all thumbs—black ones, at that—when it comes to flowers. His favorites are birds-of-paradise and poinsettia, plants we loathe as much as their sterile counterparts, plastic flowers. Watching him shove a bulb or slip into the ground, one can almost hear the last rites being intoned. After mourning several such graveside ceremonies, we made it a rule never to put anything more delicate than a shovel in his hands.

Peter seemed the ideal choice to pick up the cudgels I dropped in the chicken house. He had grown up on a farm in Holland. Surely, there must have been weekly visits to the hen house prior to Sunday's dinner. Tomorrow was Tuesday, the day Peter never failed to appear at the kitchen door at precisely the moment I was pouring coffee.

"You ought to try hot chocolate for breakfast, Mr. Colen. Much better on the nerves." He settled for his traditional cup of coffee-saturated sugar and then asked, "What's to be done today?"

"Ever kill a chicken, Peter?"

"Wish I had a dollar for every one."

"Want to kill ours?"

"You gonna pluck and clean 'em?"

"No, I'd never be able to do it as well as you."

"Okay, if that's the way you want it. Take time, you know. About forty minutes a bird. I've lost the knack. Me and my wife always buy 'em at the supermarket."

Peter was showing me who was the real, up-to-date American. Also, by "time" I knew he meant "money." Over a second cup of coffee we stopped to figure out what one decapitated, defoliated, and deboweled two-pound broiler would cost. It came to about $5.21 a head.

Peter was the one to say, "That's a darn expensive pot of soup. Why don't you give them away?" I explained that the only interested parties were the dogs and cats, and chicken bones were bad for them.

"I got a lady customer out in the Valley who's crazy like you people about animals. She'll take the ducks too. They're Republicans." The seeming *non sequitur* was Peter's highest form of praise, his way of guaranteeing the reliability of the future foster parents.

As Peter loaded the squawking gunnysacks in the back of his truck (with "America—Love It or Leave It" on the bumper) I knew the added joy of a political victory. Beginning the next morning, two members of the silent majority would start losing sleep.

Although Eszter missed Rusty and our neck exercises with the ducks, she had to confess that one of the great moments in our life was when we tore down the unsightly Maginot Line of chicken wire. Even cleaning, deodorizing, and repainting the hen house was a pleasurable experience. There were also residual joys left over from the poultry exodus. Their yard was so fertile, Eszter turned it into an auxiliary vegetable garden. The lush tomatoes, squash, green peppers, and snow peas which now grow on that recent battlefield are better than any duck egg I ever tasted. Where the filthy duck pond had been—I had inconsiderately failed to install a filter system—now stands a verdant fig whose fruit is nearly ripe. But going back to the day the wire curtain had fallen. We were wrong. The chicken battle was far from over.

Eszter still had to wear earplugs. Cornelia's rooster was now crowing twice as loud trying to establish lines of communication with the departed Rusty. Andrew claimed he was not bothered by the cacophony; however, it was mentioned at the same time that he would not be renewing the lease, which expired at the end of the month. The money he had saved by writing for others was going to be used to stake a year of writing for himself. He needed a less expensive place to house his typewriter. The next time we placed an ad for the guest house the heading would have to read "Deaf Single Only," unless the Clarkes could be persuaded to part with their flock.

Eszter tried first. Cornelia was invited down to see the newly landscaped chicken area on the theory that once the woman saw how peaceful, clean, and beautiful life could be, she would want to keep up with the Joneses, so to speak. Cornelia was impressed but hardly envious. "You must miss them something awful." Her family had never had pets before, so the chickens were as inviolate as our cats and dogs. Trading on the comparison, Eszter countered, "I know how you feel, Cornelia, but the dogs don't wake you up at five in the morning." Walking back to the fence which separated our two properties—a gate had been installed when chicken swapping was at its height—Eszter secured a promise that the rooster would be cooped up behind their house, far from the guest cottage. End of Round One.

Round Two: Squire crowed just as loudly, only it took a little longer for the sound to come our way. Informed of the acoustical fact, C pledges to put blackout cloth on Squire's cage until Colens and Smith awake naturally. Silk moiré covering to be supplied from leftovers of E.H. Collection.

Round Three: Heated battle over Eszter's habit of sleeping late. A few low blows are exchanged. Referee intercedes.

Round Four: Cornelia's husband, a professor of German, entered the ring as a reluctant co-referee. My letter to this worthy man started, "Dear Richard, RE: Squire," and went on to demonstrate with pure Hegelian logic how the existence of their one rooster would lead to Götterdämmerung. Knowing the problems of disposal, I enclosed the telephone number of Peter's Republican contact. Man to man, I postscripted a German proverb: "The god of the lucky is silence." The postman brought a return letter—the women had bolted our common gate from both sides—which was a witty balance of family loyalty and neighborly compassion.

A few mornings later, Eszter sat up in bed poking about her ears for the stoppers she had already removed. Ominous silence filled the air. Even the birds had stopped their chirping in wonderment. Tiffany's ears swept the horizon like radar cones. Eszter's face bore the same distrustful expression as when she sees Zsa Zsa Gabor on television. "Something's wrong."

"Don't be silly. They got rid of Squire. I didn't think it would be this soon."

"That's exactly what I mean. Battles aren't won that easily. Something else is bound to happen." The Americanization of Eszter has never lightened her brooding pessimism, the down position on the Hungarian seesaw of moods. But this time, three pounds of What-a-Puss were enough to push Eszter back on high, to take her mind off dark premonitions.

Unlike Kati, What-a-Puss is the antithesis of a loner. She should really be the official convention greeter for some fraternal organization, say the Kiwanis or the Knights of Columbus. I do not believe that the voices of cats or dogs sound like anything but the noises of cats and dogs, even though some of our borderline acquaintances swear that their pets speak perfect English. No dog of ours has ever said, "You put too much kibble in this food" or, "Excuse me, I have to go to the bathroom." Nevertheless, were I to play back a tape of Whatta's opening meow whenever *any* two- or four-legged creature approaches, three out of four phoneticians would agree the sound was "Hello," although they might carp about the pronunciation. Whatta accents the first syllable and then slides down a few octaves for the "lo."

With social contact established, What-a-Puss rolls over on her back in order that new friends may have a clear view of the baby-pink skin beneath the snowy white curls. She stays in that gatefold position until her stomach and bosom are rubbed, all the time making seductive, do-it-again sounds. Most cats hate being brushed and Eszter has the weekly scars to prove ours are no exception. Not What-a-Puss. As soon as she sees Eszter sit down on the terrace with her basket of brushes, combs, and talc, she rushes to the beauty salon as though important company were coming for dinner. When the session is reluctantly over, instead of scratching the hairdresser, Whatta tips her generously with appreciative purrs and licks. Tiffany, of course, is irresistibly drawn to that sweet-smelling powder and the Persian has no objections to his taking as many whiffs as he wants. In fact, she goes to great lengths to accommodate Tiffany's wishes, frequently settling her aromatic body on his sleeping back, just as the Siamese had done with Dorka. In summation, What-a-Puss's flirtatious, wanton behavior was such that we kept her under house arrest and prevailed upon Dr. Sprowl to fix the young lady a month before the normal time.

The operation had no effect upon What-a-Puss except to make her even more loving. She changed her sleeping arrangement. Instead of settling down for the night in the wicker basket Eszter had decorated with exciting colored tassels, Whatta put aside childish things and slept on our bed. More precisely, on the top of Eszter's head. In the beginning she had us all to herself, for Pancake and Petunia would have nothing to do with this Northern California interloper. They were very angry about the adoption, stayed away four or five nights in a row, and only slim pickings in the field or closed doors in the neighborhood forced them home for a quick meal and a nap. The latter took place in the back seat of the car.

From lights out until dawn What-a-Puss uses Eszter's hair

as a pillow, but at about five-thirty she gets up and does her morning exercises. These consist of standing in one place and pushing down with first the right and then the left front paw. For her calisthenics, Whatta prefers a gym mat of human skin. I say the sensation is that of having a soldier mark time on your face; Eszter likens it more to a Japanese geisha walking up and down your spine or a housewife kneading her morning dough. When all three of us are sufficiently exhausted, Whatta stops as suddenly as she began and curls up on the palm of Eszter's outstretched hand. Hours later I find them sleeping in the same position.

Nightly use of Neo-Medrol and morning applications of What-a-Puss had an insidiously soothing effect upon my psyche. I was finally hooked on cats. It was I, recalling a line heard somewhere, who said, "Vun is not enough. Every animal should grow up with a playmate."

For once, it was Eszter who had difficulty hearing. "What?"

"What-a-Puss wouldn't be kneading us to death if she had a friend her own size and age. Even if we paid them, Pancake and Petunia won't offer any companionship, that's for sure. Let's find her somebody."

Lest agreement turn conversion to apostasy, Eszter remained silent until the weekend and the arrival of the Sunday paper. Nothing in the pets-for-sale column caught her fancy. "Just a bunch of cats and dogs. But there's a cat show in Santa Monica. Want to go?"

I couldn't. The same paper carried a new ad for the guest house. Andrew had left several weeks before. "But you go. It only takes one of us to say no." Which reminded me. "Promise you'll get just one kitten for What-a-Puss."

Eszter left around noon with the cat carrier, sworn to restraint and a prompt return. By five she was not back and I was worried. At six, I was very worried. Sunday traffic around Los Angeles is not so much heavy as it is lethal. A little after seven Eszter came home. To my great surprise the cat carrier was empty and there were no unusual bulges or sounds in the area of blouse or pockets. She had that last-minute-Christmas-shopping-exhausted look and voice. "I couldn't make up my mind. You never saw so many cats and they're all looking at you with those please-take-me-home-with-you eyes. But I narrowed the choice down a bit." Out of her wallet tumbled at least a dozen cards from the various breeders with names, telephone numbers, and dates of expected kindles. On each Eszter had scribed identifying traits —i.e., "Black is beautiful," "Bushiest tail in show," "Bit my finger," or "Bitchy owner."

Remembering why I had not been along to help her make a decision at the show, Eszter asked, "You have any better luck today?"

"Maybe. A very nice woman called and—"

"I thought we agreed, no more women."

"She was calling for her boss. Seemed most interested in how private the place was. I told her like an unlisted telephone number. She's bringing him up tomorrow."

"I wonder what he does."

"She said he's 'in the business.'"

"Oh, my God. Let's hope it's not an actor."

Monday nights are my turn to cook. That particular day was selected on the theory that after weekends of too much to eat, an occasional skipped course or even total fasting would do no harm. Eszter pulled a stool up to the chopping block to keep me company. "We're going to get along fine."

"You're only saying that because I'm such a good cook."

"That's true, but I meant Steve and us."

"Steve?"

"McQueen. He's the one the woman called about. They were up this afternoon. He loved the place and is moving in next week."

"Except for Gary Cooper, I thought you didn't like actors."

"I don't, but he's a man. And very nice. He even apologized for the fact that he doesn't sleep well, so if we should meet in the morning and he's grumpy, it's his metabolism."

As far as Eszter was concerned, our tenant-to-be could not have found a more civilized or simpatico thing to say. The most thoughtful and lasting of our wedding presents had been a bedside clock from Eszter's sister inscribed: "Bruce dear: For a long and happy marriage, don't talk to her before breakfast. Love, Zsoka." She forgot to engrave what time her sister had breakfast. Ten-thirty.

With the guest house problem seemingly solved, we went back to finding a roomer for What-a-Puss. Eszter spread out her cat-show cards by the kitchen phone and contacted each breeder from San Diego to Santa Barbara, making appointments to inspect their wares. Dozens of phone calls and one thousand miles later, she made her final choice—an eight-week-old male Himalayan. Ironically, the breeder lived five minutes away in Benedict Canyon. His first evening at our home, the new cat spent so much time bouncing back and forth on the bed inspecting Eszter and myself, bringing his personnel files up to date, that we called him Ping-Pong.

What-a-Puss was demonstratively pleased with her new companion. Ping-Pong, clearly, would have been her own stag-line choice. She met him in the front hall, said hello, and stretched out in her languid, ain't-I-something pose. Ping moved cautiously forward and then, pong, they were in each other's arms, rolling over and over exchanging love bites at every turn. After the strenuous reception, Eszter placed Ping-Pong in the bassinet, hoping that he would be the bait to get Whatta back in the habit of sleeping where she belonged. The latter did pop in but only long enough to persuade Ping-Pong that our bed was far roomier and, what with the electric blanket, warmer. What-a-Puss still kneads, by the way, although not quite as much, for now one third of her morning pushups are conducted on Ping-Pong's cushiony, always full stomach.

Ping-Pong did more than fill the gap in Whatta's life; he prevailed upon Pancake and Petunia to forget their petty jealousy and rejoin the fold. Ping was ideally made for the role of intermediary, for Himalayans are half Siamese, half Persian. They have the coloration of the first, the long billowy hair of the second. Maybe the two deserters, seeing the choco-

late-dipped face, ears, and paws of the latest passenger to
check aboard the ark, recognized a half brother and decided
if he could put up with What-a-Puss, perhaps they should
give it a try. Besides, it was still the best restaurant in town.
Whichever the reason, Pancake and Petunia slowly, very
slowly, made their way back into the house and when nobody was looking settled down on the electric counterpane,
which Management still kept at "low" twenty-four hours a
day. Now they both return to the bedroom each evening, cast
anti-long-hair looks in Whatta's direction, but make a big thing
of kissing bushy Ping-Pong goodnight. What-a-Puss couldn't
care less. She knows that in the Persian half of Ping-Pong lies
his heart and it is sworn to her.

Ping-Pong's role of pacifier extends to the adult world. He
is a purring garbage disposal of life's pressures. If one or a
dozen worried thoughts are zinging about the room, Ping has
the capacity to slurp them down to a pea-size pulp of trivia.
I am not quite sure how he does it, but when the grinding up
is going on, I have noticed that his long white whiskers bristle,
his eyebrows touch the end of his nose, and his whole face
takes on a determined, bulldog look. It must be very hard
work, this shredding of other people's worries, for after exor-
cising the evil spirits, Ping-Pong drags himself to the nearest
pillow and sleeps for five or six hours. Unfortunately, Ping's
therapeutic gifts were unable to cope with the metabolism
crisis which occurred the morning after Steve moved in.

14

Star Power

Betsy, Steve's polite private secretary–public fixer-upper, called at about eight-thirty. "Good morning, Mr. Colen, I hope I didn't wake you up, but Mr. McQueen called me two hours ago. He wondered if you had noticed the presence of wildlife in the neighborhood."

Andrew had found the bridge blocked by a rattlesnake, and bees had built a magnificent four-by-five-foot hive around the front door of the guest house, but those tenants had been evicted long ago. "Was Tiffany barking?"

"Oh no, Mr. Colen, Mr. McQueen said it was more like a cackling noise coming from behind his house. It woke him up at six o'clock and went on and on and on. Could there be chickens in your vicinity?"

I said I would take care of the matter. A good example of morning bravado, for not only had we not spoken to the Clarkes since Rusty's excommunication, but ivy now covered the gate and its two locks. I once was a great admirer of Robert Frost's lovely poem about fences making good neighbors, but as a homeowner I have come to realize that the verse has a gaping weakness: In every fence there has to be a gate.

Betsy finished her report with the plea, "You won't mention Mr. McQueen's name, I hope?"

She need not have worried. Steve's one reservation about renting the place reflected our single worry about leasing it to him. He did not want anyone to know where he lived in fear that the hounders of movie stars—autograph fans, press agents, movie magazine editors, gossip columnists, etc.— would flush him out. On our part there were visions of the gate being stormed by squealing teeny-boppers, of the wall itself being gradually chipped to nothing by memento seekers, and of the driveway being choked with caravans delivering Special Delivery letters, telegrams, and heart-shaped pillows with "I Love You Stevie" embroidered on them. Since our mutual concerns canceled out, we swore each other to secrecy for the length of the lease. Is there any point in recording what Eszter said when I told her that her premonition had been correct?

The calls to the Clarkes started anew. It was one thing to ask for the removal of a rooster, another to suggest that their whole flock be put on the block. To curb any display of sluggish metabolism, I stood by while Eszter phoned Cornelia to explain that we had a new tenant whose ears were more sensitive than Andrew's. This time Eszter wasn't asking for herself but on behalf of a fellow insomniac. When Eszter put down the receiver, I asked, "What did she say?"

"She'll move the hens as far away from the fence line as possible."

"How did she sound?"

"Distant."

The following morning, Eszter broke her never-before-ten rule by sneaking out to the bridge at seven to listen if the hens could still be heard hawking their wares. They could. In confirmation of her findings, Steve was pacing back and forth on the porch deck. Landlady and tenant tightened the cords on their bathrobes and had a conference. Very apologetically, Steve related the difficulties he had in getting to sleep and that one reason he had been attracted to the place was that it seemed so quiet and peaceful.

"You know, Eszter, maybe I could get used to the damn chickens, but she talks to them. Once they've laid, the woman coos and clucks and tells them she's never seen such a big, beautiful egg. Christ."

Eszter apologized. She knew just what he was going through and would see that something was done. After comparing notes on the relative merits of sleeping pills, night shades, mystery books, and earplugs, she returned to the house and picked up the phone.

"Eszter, don't you want to eat something first?"

"Which do you want me to lose, my courage or my breakfast?"

I picked up the extension in the other room. The only handicap to eavesdropping is the inability to interrupt.

"Hello, Cornelia. Sorry to call you at this ungodly hour, but it's important."

"Oh, hi there, Eszter. I've been up for hours."

"Well, that's sort of why I'm calling. Our tenant still hears you and the chickens in the morning."

There followed the pause that depresses.

"What kind of people are you renting to down there, anyway? Haven't they ever heard birds before?"

"It's a he, Cornelia, and chickens aren't birds. Oh, you know what I mean. A person can get used to bird birds."

"Eszter, Number One, the hens have been moved way beyond our house. I can't understand why he hears anything. Number Two, I don't want to talk about it anymore."

"Well, Number Three, I do. Heard them myself this morning. Or maybe it's you down there doing the cackling under his window?"

I do not know who hung up second, because I was first. Richard was off on a lecture tour, or more rational minds might have again solved the problem. A call to the Department of Animal Regulations settled what I had never bothered checking when we were in the poultry business: pet-wise, the area was zoned for chickens. I explained my problem to a harried L.A. police sergeant, asking if that did not constitute Disturbing the Peace. "Mister, when you hear somebody yell Rape, Murder, or Holdup, that's disturbing the peace. A couple of lousy squawking hens? You don't know when you're lucky." Our lawyer said what all lawyers say: We didn't have a leg to stand on.

Steve got paler and paler, the noise of his Porsche leaving at 8:00 A.M. became louder and louder, and his crooked, sexy smile straightened out to a thin line of pain. He began spending Fridays to Mondays in Palm Springs, sleeping.

While the Second Chicken War raged on, I was trying to write this book. "Trying" is the only word, for between supplicating phone calls from Steve and Betsy, Eszter's hourly reports from the front lines and What-a-Puss's new habit of sitting on my study desk, auditioning for the ingenue role in *The Boy Friend*, somewhere between 100 and 102 words were being written each day. I needed a retreat, a spartan cell free of distractions, empty of all the convenient excuses not to work, like: a library to leaf through, pictures to stare at, animals to play with, a phone to dial, a nearby kitchen to plunder, or a couch to nap on. Eszter suggested the playhouse-turned-toolhouse-turned-chicken-coop.

White paint, beaverboard panels, and a tile floor hid all signs, but one, of the former occupants. On the wall directly above my typewriter was nailed the "Push" sign which had once inspired productivity of another sort. The perfect office, but to remove the slightly monastic feeling, and because no writer should be cut off from the outside world, I put up bookshelves, hung pictures, squeezed an army cot in the six-by-eight-foot space, and had a phone installed. I remember particularly when the last was accomplished.

Out of purely horticultural curiosity, Eszter was tending some marijuana plants. The seeds were wafted this way from Acapulco and had sown themselves behind a curtain of cornstalks and sunflowers. When they peeked above this natural hedge and were within helicopter range, they were ready for harvest. One day I noticed fifteen to twenty bundles of leaves, neatly tied and gathered with red yarn, dangling from the clothesline. After my fifth recital of the criminal penalties for hanging this sort of wash out in public, Eszter reluctantly agreed—"They use it to cure the common cold in Canada"—to find a more hidden spot for the medicinal nosegays. I discovered where when the telephone man said to me, "I put your new extension where the pot was hanging. That okay?"

Through one window of my new quarters I could see the flower gardens cozying up to the main house and watch the transient trade at the Zhivago bird sanctuary. Out the other was a view of the orchard and, with the door held ajar by *The American Heritage Dictionary* (with the 1971 earthquake, the chicken house listed about fifteen degrees), I could see a family of deer grazing on the wild hillside across the way. To make up for what Nature watching and native procrastination were doing to my word output, I was forced to wedge myself under the typewriter at six each morning, seven days a week. About seven-thirty on a Sunday morning, six weeks after Steve had moved in, the new telephone rang. I was sure it was someone in New York; they are always getting confused about whether it is three hours earlier or later in California.

"Hello?"

"Hi, Bruce, this is Steve." He sounded Bullitt-angry.

"Morning. I thought you were in Palm Springs."

"I had to stay here." Home, sweet home. "Listen, we gotta do something. I slept exactly three hours. I'm ready to climb over that fence and shoot those goddamn miserable chickens."

"Steve, I'm sorry. I've called our lawyer, the animal regulation people and—"

"So did I."

"Maybe when her husband comes back I can get somewhere."

"Bruce, I don't want to spoil the good vibrations between us, but I can't wait, I won't go through another morning of this

chicken shit." He was so desperate, I never thought to laugh.
"Does she know I live here?"

"No."

"Well, what do you think if I just go up there and lay it on
the line?"

"Maybe. Let me see what Eszter thinks. She's still asleep.
I'll call you back."

As I put down the phone, the window shade went up on
our bedroom window. Steve's call had rousted all his allies.
Before telling Eszter the latest, I brought her orange juice,
a thyroid pill, and coffee. Our strategy session called for clear
heads. We both agreed that given the choice of Steve's keeping his anonymity or his sanity, we opted for his health.
Eszter was reaching for the bedside phone to tell him to go
visit Cornelia, when it rang.

"Morning, Steve. Bruce just told me." She gestured madly
toward the study. I ran to pick up the party line. Steve
sounded as though he had just won an Academy Award.

"Yeah, I couldn't hold myself back any longer."

I heard Eszter interrupt the narrative to ask what he was
wearing.

"A bathrobe. I jumped over the fence [it's six feet high]
and ran up to their house. You know those sliding doors by
the pool? Well, I banged on those until this woman came out
in her bathrobe and curlers." Now Eszter had the whole fashion picture. "A long-haired boy was with her."

"Were they surprised? What did she say?"

"I guess so. I was so riled up that as soon as she opened the
door, I did the talking. I said, 'I'm Steve McQueen and I
apologize for climbing your fence, but I live in the Colens'
guest house and I can't sleep with your chickens clucking all
the time. Will you please get rid of them? It's very unfair of
you.' I was very polite, Eszter."

"I'm sure you were. Then what did she say?"

"She sort of covered the curlers with her hand and said,
'I'm very sorry, Mr. McQueen, I'd get rid of them, but it's
really up to my son. He raised them from chicks.' The boy

looked at his mother like he'd just been sold down the river. At first he said no, so I took him for a walk around the pool. I can rap pretty good with kids, you know. We talked about motorbikes, his girl, and Vietnam. Anyway, he said yes, too. If you don't see me for a couple of days it's because I'm sleeping." Steve was able to start his period of hibernation by noontime, for Cornelia and her son kept their word that promptly.

On V-E day, 1945, I was an office boy trapped in the mail room of Simon & Schuster. On V-J day I was still glued to the same stamp machine, while my letter-writing superiors were out celebrating. On Sunday, November 21, 1971, with clear conscience, I made up for all the missed victory revelry. Shakespeare, *Henry I*, Part IV: "Nothing can seem foul to those that win."

15

The Missing Hapsburg Look

With Steve happily tucked in bed enjoying the reign of silence, we no longer jumped when the telephone rang or bickered about who had to pick it up next. To confirm the fact that the instrument might once again announce good news, the Seeing Eye breeder called and said we could pick up our Alsatian. In five minutes, Eszter rounded up Tiffany, I found my wallet, and the three of us were on our way.

The kennel was hidden among the deserted hills behind Malibu. The reason for the deliberate seclusion was frighteningly apparent the moment we stepped out of the car and several dozen German shepherds barked a salute.

As Eszter tied Tiffany's leash to the armrest—we are on our third—she reassured him: "Don't worry, Tiff, we'll be right back with our new burglar alarm."

Walking down the aisle separating the dog runs, I had the feeling we were reviewing a razor-sharp, beautifully groomed honor guard. But each dog was violating the "eyes front" command. Their heads turned in cadence with our steps as we moved by. *They* were doing the inspecting. The trainer's wife was taking us on this tour. Her husband was out schooling a blind girl and her new shepherd at a busy shopping center. Nearing the last run, staccato barks gave way to yaps and yelps. Five black puppies were playing pyramid, the object of the game being to see which one could climb on top of the other four and stay there the longest. Mrs. Schmidt reached into the base of this squirming pile and woke up the chubbiest of the lot. One flapping ear was at half-mast, the other fell forward covering one of his warm, wet brown eyes, Veronica Lake style. The rest was all stomach, black curls, and huge, flat feet. When he stopped yawning, Eszter kissed him on the nose and said to Mrs. Schmidt, by way of a reminder, "Your husband promised me the pick of the litter."

"Ya, das is dee vune."

All of a sudden, Eszter's English became impeccable. "Surely you know better than I, but he looks a little different from his brothers and sisters."

"Das is because he is more *Mann*. Even in the Vaterland, I have never seen a more better vune. Ven you vill see his papers, Frau, you vill see da pure German line."

Without looking at Eszter, I thought this sounded like the right moment to take our black Aryan puppy and leave. "Thank you very much, Mrs. Schmidt. I hope you understand, we must take the dog to our vet for a checkup on the way home. So this check will read 'Subject to vet's approval,' okay?"

"Ya, of course, dat dog is sound as a Deutsche mark, a real champion. A man from Japan offered my husband twelve thousand dollars for his grandfather." I gathered from Mrs. Schmidt that Japanese ingenuity had gotten around to photographing the Annual Reports of Purina, Gaines, and other canine victualers. They found that the friends of man's best friend were backing their affection with hundreds of millions of dollars each year. To gain acceptance in this big money crowd, the Japanese were top bidders for champion stock, here and in Europe. The day cannot be far off when we will be able to buy Pearl Harbor Yummies, Kamikaze Kibble, or Hiroshima Atomic Flea Collars. Mrs. Schmidt ended her digression and, once again, reassured us, "If dere's something the matter mit dat dog, ever, you bring him back. We give you back your dollars."

Tiffany and the big black ball were instant pals. All the way to Sprowl's they played two-handed pyramid in the back seat. Taking the weight and age of his opponent into consideration, Tiff threw almost every game. Actually, we thought it highly unlikely that there was anything physically wrong with this shiny-coated, bouncing puppy. The clinic's receptionist summed up our true concern. "Gosh, he's cute. What is he, a Labrador?"

I had less difficulty answering the next question, "What's his name?"

"Gibbs."

"Would you mind spelling that?"

"Capital *G*, period, capital *B*, period, capital *S*, period."

Remembering the deferred status of our income, it seemed improvident to touch savings to pay for What-a-Puss, Ping-Pong, and now "What is he?" I sold an original drawing of George Bernard Shaw, done by S. J. Woolf for the cover of the *New York Times Magazine* section. Below the extraordinary likeness was pasted a letter from Shaw to Woolf explaining that he was very busy and that his terms for sitting would be "$3,500 an hour." In the late forties, I had found this rare bit of Shaviana mixed in with an exhibition of some not very good antiques at a Parke-Bernet exhibition. The afternoon of the auction, New York was in the midst of an attendance-dampening rainstorm. GBS was knocked down for $35. As one of England's most eloquent antivivisectionists, Shaw, I like to think, would have been pleased with what we did with the profit earned from his portrait.

Dr. Sprowl was washing his hands after the examination. "That's a very healthy dog. One of his testicles hasn't descended yet, but even if it doesn't, that's nothing to worry about unless you plan to breed or show him."

Neither interested us, but I asked, "What would we show him as, Doctor?"

Sprowl was unsuccessful in suppressing a laugh. "That's a question. From what you say about his breeding, he should be a shepherd; but sometimes, even in the best of families, there are throwbacks." He ran his hand along the ridge of Gibbs's nose. "It should be longer; his eyes should have more fire in them. He just doesn't seem to have that Hapsburg look. You know what I mean?"

This time Eszter laughed, and then asked, "All I care about, Doctor, do you think we can train him to be a guard dog?"

"Too early to tell, Mrs. Colen. Anyway, you wouldn't want to start training him till he's a year old. Right now, all I can say is that you have a very intelligent dog with an unusually sweet disposition." Gibbs shifted his eyes from Sprowl to us, as though checking to see if that was sufficient.

On the way out I repeated to Dr. Sprowl the terms of Mrs. Schmidt's money-back guarantee. He became visibly annoyed for the first time since we had known him. "Mr. Colen, that's the safest warranty any seller ever dreamed up. Would you return this puppy six months from now if we found out he had a serious hereditary disease? Of course not. I'll bet you wouldn't even take him back now. And how long have you had it, two hours? Dog buyers need a Betty Furness."

Driving home, Eszter held G.B.S. in her lap and reviewed the situation. "If Gibbs's ears go up, his testicle comes down, his nose grows longer, and his hair shorter, we may have an Alsatian."

In only one respect did G.B.S. act as though he had the mistaken notion that he might be on probation: he became completely house-trained in two weeks. A house record. Of course I am not counting his reflex of urinating on the kitchen tiles when he came to kiss Eszter and me good morning. The excitement of love is forgivable. Until he managed to control his ardor, we scheduled these diurnal meetings for the terrace. What Gibbs saved us on rug shampoos, he squandered ten times over in other areas. For whatever he was destined to become, during those first few months the black sheep of the Hapsburg line was a plain old puppy in every destructive sense of the word.

A *Schöngeist* from the word no, Gibbs threw his whole being into Nature watching. As far as he was concerned, a flower bed was just that—something to lie down in. And if at first the bed felt a little uncomfortable—and it always did—then scratching and rolling about got rid of the bumps. Out came the used chicken wire; up went the look-but-don't-touch barrier. Shut out from these pastoral pleasures, Gibbs discovered my prize lemon tree halfway up the drive and the limb-sagging crop of yellow balls which dangled within jumping reach. With a yellow sphere in his mouth he goes to the top of the driveway, opens his jaws, and chases the rolling ball down to the gate. I have tried substituting every variety of dime-store ball, but Gibbs finds these flavorless and they roll too fast and too straight. His appreciation for Nature's playthings includes the supposedly poisonous fruit of Jerusalem cherry bushes. Gibbs wanders about until he has picked off a mouthful of them and then settles down on the lawn to nose and mash his collection of red marbles. The dog's ability to keep busy without organized play would be most commendable were it not that he discovered toys indoors as well as out.

Every morning, before turning on the lawn sprinklers, we can expect to retrieve any or all of the following: sunglasses, with or without case; pillows without stuffing; belts with new holes punched in them; fingerless garden gloves; and unrolled rolls of paper towels, the 120-square-foot brand. In more secret spots, we have found Eszter's cigarettes, my pipes, and boxes of kitchen matches. The last can be forgiven as normal boyhood curiosity and the lawn debris seems to be lessening now that Gibbs is almost seven months old and nearing the end of his teething period but the dog's persistent shoe fetish has me worried.

Finding that the shoes on our feet had an unfriendly habit

of walking away, he set about building up his own collection. Gibbs's half of the doghouse mat looks like the "Unclaimed" shelf in a cobbler's shop. Except for an occasional lace, he shows no interest in chewing up the pilfered sneakers, slippers, shoes, sandals, and his favorite, boots. The dog's pleasure lies in just looking, and periodically sniffing, this wonderfully stimulating array of footwear. He sleeps with his head pillowed on Eszter's yellow garden boots. Friends have gotten used to the fact that the Colens frequently hobble about in one shoe, looking for the other; and one recent guest has called several times to inquire if we have found the left pump "which slipped off my foot under the dinner table." Why do we not cut off Gibbs's illicit supply of erotic toys by simply shutting all doors? Because there is an eight-by-twelve-inch hole in our house which cannot be sealed—the cat door, at the bottom of the Dutch door in the kitchen.

This flapping rubber entrance presents the same problem faced by the membership committee of certain private clubs: how can we let some in and keep others out? In this case, the cats pass; Gibbs is the undesirable element. None of the Danes have ever tried pushing their way in where they were not wanted, although Dorka did have a nightly habit of squeezing her head through the hole to smell what was cooking. If we seal off the pet entrance, barring Gibbs, and leave open the top half of the door so that the cats can reach their tray of liver on the kitchen floor, then the flies come in to nibble the food and the mosquitoes to sample us. Further complicating the arrangement is the fact that since the cats sleep in our bedroom, the inner door between kitchen and living room must be left ajar until they retire. It is Gibbs's position that anywhere a Siamese goes, he can go too. Using his short nose as a wedge, the door which was slightly ajar is opened wide.

For a brief moment I once thought the solution to the conundrum was to install a second, smaller pet flap in the interior door. That way Gibbs would be limited to stealing the cats' food and a few pot holders, but Eszter reminded me why another pet door solved nothing. Until What-a-Puss and Ping-Pong were ten months old, mature enough to cope with the outside world, they had to be kept indoors from dusk to dawn. Therefore, at night, if "someone" should forget to close the bedroom door after letting in Pancake and Petunia, then What-a-Puss and Ping-Pong would escape through "someone's" second pet door and be eaten up by coyotes.

For those who are still with me, I am sure the solution to this puzzle is quite obvious. I should have bought a smaller pet door in the first place or a bigger Alsatian in the second. To do the first now, means buying a whole new three-inch-thick Dutch door and who is bold enough to say that someday we may not have a new cat-size dog? As for changing Gibbs?

Never. We all love him much too much. His genital problem is still up in the air, his hair has not grown shorter but is falling out by the handful and any minor lengthening of his snout comes from prying open doors and getting his nose caught in the toes of shoes. Blind Tiffany's love for Gibbs is touchingly total. He allows the black woolly bear to chew his ears, jowls, and neck until they are raw and then it is *he* who initiates the make-up kisses which follow. Or when Gibbs provokes a half-hour no-holds-barred fight on the lawn, the aging Dane obliges. As a result of this forced exercise, Tiffany has never looked better. No, Gibbs is here to stay; but we both keep hunting for an alternative to the messy, annoying game of musical doors which we are constantly forced to play.

A night or so ago, while embroidering, Eszter confessed a solution that had been formulating in her mind. She was nearly finished with her first non-flower design. It is of What-a-Puss at the zenith of a yawn, that eyes-shut, mouth-open moment when the cat looks most as though she were laughing. What-a-Puss sat on a nearby cushion, anxious to see, like every other model, if the artist had captured "the real me." Eszter went right on working while she talked.

"You know, if Gibbs's ears would only stick up the way they should, maybe he wouldn't be able to get through the cat door."

At times, his left ear stands proud and erect, but the right has rarely made it. Once or twice I have seen both fully elevated while he slept. Whether these rare moments are the result of a compensatory dream or the downward angle of his head, I do not know. Most of the time the huge flapping flags are snagged halfway up the pole. When seen like this, ears folded in half, Gibbs looks as though he is wearing a bullfighter's *montera*. "I've given up in that department. Actually, I sort of like them the way they are. He looks so friendly and sweet."

"That's exactly what we wanted—a friendly, cute guard dog. It's really my fault."

"Don't be silly. Look at his pedigree. Have you ever seen such a ferocious, Teutonic-sounding list of ancestors?"

"Oh, I don't mean Gibbs. Having an attack dog around would be much too dangerous, anyway. I'm talking about the house. It was remodeled all wrong. I never gave a thought to the comings and goings of the animals. Instead of a pet door, what our cats and dogs need is a room of their own."

I thought we were only supposing, so I asked where.

"We could turn the garage into a big communal living-kitchen. Have a huge tile stove in the corner, built-in bunks for the animals, a brick floor so we wouldn't have to worry about them tracking in dirt. Tables and chairs for ourselves. It would keep the rest of the house clean and we could break through that one wall which faces my studio. I'd get a lot more work done, if they were around."

"You forgot a shoe rack for Gibbs. That's a very expensive little remodeling job."

"I hereby assign all royalties from the new What-a-Puss Kit to the project."

"What about the car?"

"That. What's more important, that the animals have a roof over their head, or the car getting a little dirty? The rainy season is a long way off. Maybe by then there'll be a Ping-Pong Kit to pay for a carport."

Quite obviously, the resident designer had done a great

deal of thinking about this. It was time I mentioned a few things she had forgotten. "What about the kitchen we have now?"

"We'll turn that into a wonderful, spacious office for you. You don't want to write in a chicken coop all your life."

"I like it out there. The place reminds me that things could always be worse than they are."

"Okay, then the kitchen could be a combination sauna and bar. You've always wanted both. It's got a great view and all the pipes are already there."

"And the doghouse?"

"That's for me. It faces south and would made a perfect solarium–potting shed." Eszter put down her embroidery and picked up the pad and pencil she normally uses to record the amounts and colors of yarn used in each needlepainting. "I better make a note of the number of bunks we'll need in the new room. I'm adding two extra. Pretty soon we'll just have to get a boy and girl harlequin. Don't you think?"

I went out to the doghouse and had my first cigarette since falling off the roof.